PHYSICS

Arthur Eisenkraft, Ph.D.

Active Physics has been developed in association
with the
American Association of Physics Teachers (AAPT)
and the
American Institute of Physics (AIP)

Published by
IT'S ABOUT TIME, Inc.
Armonk, NY

Published in 1998 by

It's About Time, Inc.
84 Business Park Drive Armonk, NY 10504
Phone (914) 273-2233 Fax (914) 273-2227
Toll Free (888) 698-TIME
http://Its-About-Time.com

Publisher
Laurie Kreindler

Project Manager
Ruta Demery

Design
John Nordland

Project Associate
Nancy Uhl

Video Production
Barbara Zahm

Creative Artwork
Tomas Bunk

Cover Illustration
Steven Belcher

Technical Art
Darmouth Publishing, Inc.

Illustrations and Photos

Chapter 1: Tomas Bunk pages 4,10, 17, 22, 26, 40 & 46; ©Ford Photomedia pages 3 &13; Michael Gadomski/PhotoReseachers; Corel page 44; Nick Gunderson/Tony Stone. Chapter 2: Tomas Bunk pages 62, 67, 73, 76, 79, 84, 89, 93, 95, 100; page 59 & 60 Nicholas Pinturas/Tony Stone; page 64 AP Photos; page 69 Aldo Torelli/Tony Stone; page 83 Donald Johnston/Tony Stone. Chapter 3: Tomas Bunk pages 107, 110, 124, 134, 142, 148, 153 & 157; NASA photos pages 122, 135, 136, 138, 139, 145, 159; Royal Observatory, Edinburgh/PhotoResearchers; NASA/PhotoResearchers; Star Trek©1991 Paramount Pictures. All other photos PhotoDisc©1998.

This project was supported, in part,
by the
National Science Foundation
Opinions expressed are those of the authors
and not necessarily those of the Foundation

Transportation
Table of Contents

Acknowledgments

Project Director

Arthur Eisenkraft teaches physics and serves as science coordinator in the Bedford Public Schools in N.Y. Dr. Eisenkraft is the author of numerous science and educational publications. He holds a US Patent for a laser vision testing system and was featured in *Scientific American*.

Dr. Eisenkraft is chair of the Duracell Science Scholarship Competition; chair of the Toyota TAPESTRY program giving grants to science teachers; and chair of the Toshiba/NSTA ExploraVisions Awards competition for grades K-12. He is co-author of a contest column and serves on the advisory board of *Quantum* magazine, a collaborative effort of the US and Russia. In 1993, he served as Executive Director for the XXIV International Physics Olympiad after being Academic Director for the United States Team for six years. He served on the content committee and helped write the National Science Education Standards of the NRC (National Research Council).

Dr. Eisenkraft received the Presidential Award for Excellence in Science Teaching at the White House in 1986, and the AAPT Distinguished Service Citation for "excellent contributions to the teaching of physics" in 1989. In 1991 he was recognized by the Disney Corporation as Science Teacher of the Year in their American Teacher Awards program. In 1993 he received an Honorary Doctor of Science degree from Rensselaer Polytechnic Institute.

Primary and Contributing Authors

Transportation

Ernest Kuehl
Lawrence High School
Cedarhurst, NY

Robert L. Lehrman
Bayside, NY

Salvatore Levy
Roslyn High School
Roslyn, NY

Tom Liao
SUNY Stony Brook
Stony Brook, NY

Bob Ritter
University of Alberta
Edmonton, AB, CA

Communications

Richard Berg
University of Maryland
College Park, MD

Ron DeFronzo
Eastbay Ed. Collaborative
Attleboro, MA

Harry Rheam
Eastern Senior High School
Atco, NJ

John Roeder
The Calhoun School
New York, NY

Patty Rourke
Potomac School
McLean, VA

Larry Weathers
The Bromfield School
Harvard, MA

Home

Jon L. Harkness
Active Physics Regional Coordinator
Wausau, WI

Douglas A. Johnson
Madison West High School
Madison, WI

John J. Rusch
University of Wisconsin, Superior
Superior, WI

Medicine

Russell Hobbie
University of Minnesota
St. Paul, MN

Terry Goerke
Hill-Murray High School
St. Paul, MN

John Koser
Wayzata High School
Plymouth, MN

Ed Lee
WonderScience, Associate Editor
Silver Spring, MD

Predictions

Ruth Howes
Ball State University
Muncie, IN

Chris Chiaverina
New Trier Township High School
Crystal Lake, IL

Charles Payne
Ball State University
Muncie, IN

Ceanne Tzimopoulos
Omega Publishing
Medford, MA

Sports

Howard Brody
University of Pennsylvania
Philadelphia, PA

Mary Quinlan
Radnor High School
Radnor, PA

Carl Duzen
Lower Merion High School
Havertown, PA

Jon L. Harkness
Active Physics Regional Coordinator
Wausau, WI

David Wright
Tidewater Comm. College
Virginia Beach, VA

Principal Investigators

Bernard V. Khoury
American Association of Physics
Teachers

Dwight Edward Neuenschwander
American Institute of Physics

Consultants

Peter Brancazio
Brooklyn College of CUNY
Brooklyn, NY

Robert Capen
Canyon del Oro High School
Tucson, AZ

Jim Connolly
JK Associates
New York, NY

Carole Escobar

Earl Graf
SUNY Stony Brook
Stony Brook, NY

Jack Hehn
American Association of
Physics Teachers
College Park, MD

Donald F. Kirwan
Louisiana State University
Baton Rouge, LA

Gayle Kirwan
Louisiana State University
Baton Rouge, LA

James La Porte
Virginia Tech
Blacksburg, VA

Charles Misner
University of Maryland
College Park, MD

Robert F. Neff
Suffern, NY

Ingrid Novodvorsky
Mountain View High School
Tucson, AZ

John Robson
University of Arizona
Tucson, AZ

Mark Sanders
Virginia Tech
Blacksburg, VA

Brian Schwartz
Brooklyn College of CUNY
New York, NY

Bruce Seiger
Wellesley High School
Newburyport, MA

Clifford Swartz
SUNY Stony Brook
Setauket, NY

Barbara Tinker
The Concord Consortium
Concord, MA

Robert E. Tinker
The Concord Consortium
Concord, MA

Joyce Weiskopf
Herndon, VA

Donna Willis
American Association of
Physics Teachers
College Park, MD

Safety Reviewer

Gregory Puskar
University of West Virginia
Morgantown, WV

Equity Reviewer

Leo Edwards
Fayettville State University
Fayettville, NC

Spreadsheet and MBL

Ken Appel
Yorktown High School
Peekskill, NY

Physics at Work

Barbara Zahm
Zahm Productions
New York, NY

Physics InfoMall

Brian Adrian
Bethany College
Lindsborg, KS

Unit Reviewers

George A. Amann
F.D. Roosevelt High School
Rhinebeck, NY

Patrick Callahan
Catasaugua High School
Center Valley, PA

Beverly Cannon
Science and Engineering
Magnet High School
Dallas, TX

Barbara Chauvin

Elizabeth Chesick
The Baldwin School
Haverford, PA 19041

Chris Chiaverina
New Trier Township High School
Crystal Lake, IL

Andria Erzberger
Palo Alto Senior High School
Los Altos Hills, CA

Elizabeth Farrell Ramseyer
Niles West High School
Skokie, IL

Mary Gromko
President of Council of State
Science Supervisors
Denver, CO

Thomas Guetzloff

Jon L. Harkness
Active Physics Regional Coordinator
Wausau, WI

Dawn Harman
Moon Valley High School
Phoenix, AZ

James Hill
Piner High School
Sonoma, CA

Bob Kearney

Claudia Khourey-Bowers
McKinley Senior High School

Steve Kliewer
Bullard High School
Fresno, CA

Ernest Kuehl
Roslyn High School
Cedarhurst, NY

Jane Nelson
University High School
Orlando, FL

John Roeder
The Calhoun School
New York, NY

Patty Rourke
Potomac School
McLean, VA

Gerhard Salinger
Fairfax, VA

Irene Slater
La Pietra School for Girls

Pilot Test Teachers

John Agosta

Donald Campbell
Portage Central High School
Portage, MI

John Carlson
Norwalk Community
Technical College
Norwalk, CT

Veanna Crawford
Alamo Heights High School
New Braunfels

Janie Edmonds
West Milford High School
Randolph, NJ

Eddie Edwards
Amarillo Area Center for
Advanced Learning
Amarillo, TX

Arthur Eisenkraft
Fox Lane High School
Ossining, NY

Tom Ford

Bill Franklin

Roger Goerke
St. Paul, MN

Tom Gordon
Greenwich High School
White Plains, NY

Ariel Hepp

John Herrman
College of Steubenville
Steubenville, OH

Linda Hodges

Ernest Kuehl
Lawrence High School
Cedarhurst, NY

Fran Leary
Troy High School
Schenectady, NY

Harold Lefcourt

Cherie Lehman
West Lafayette High School
West Lafayette, IN

Kathy Malone
Shady Side Academy
Pittsburgh, PA

Bill Metzler
Westlake High School
Thornwood, NY

Elizabeth Farrell Ramseyer
Niles West High School
Skokie, IL

Daniel Repogle
Central Noble High School
Albion, IN

Evelyn Restivo
Maypearl High School
Maypearl, TX

Doug Rich
Fox Lane High School
Bedford, NY

John Roeder
The Calhoun School
New York, NY

Tom Senior
New Trier Township High School
Highland Park, IL

John Thayer
District of Columbia Public Schools
Silver Spring, MD

Carol-Ann Tripp
Providence Country Day
East Providence, RI

Yvette Van Hise
High Tech High School
Freehold, NJ

Jan Waarvick

Sandra Walton
Dubuque Senior High School
Dubuque, IA

Larry Wood
Fox Lane High School
Bedford, NY

Field Test Coordinator

Marilyn Decker
Northeastern University
Acton, MA

Field Test Workshop Staff

John Carlson

Marilyn Decker

Arthur Eisenkraft

Douglas Johnson

John Koser

Ernest Kuehl

Mary Quinlan

Elizabeth Farrell Ramseyer

John Roeder

Field Test Evaluators

Susan Baker-Cohen

Susan Cloutier

George Hein

Judith Kelley

all from Lesley College,
Cambridge, MA

Field Test Teachers and Schools

Rob Adams
Polytech High School
Woodside, DE

Benjamin Allen
Falls Church High School
Falls Church, VA

Robert Applebaum
New Trier High School
Winnetka, IL

Joe Arnett
Plano Sr. High School
Plano, TX

Bix Baker
GFW High School
Winthrop, MN

Debra Beightol
Fremont High School
Fremont, NE

Patrick Callahan
Catasaugua High School
Catasaugua, PA

George Coker
Bowling Green High School
Bowling Green, KY

Janice Costabile
South Brunswick High School
Monmouth Junction, NJ

Stanley Crum
Homestead High School
Fort Wayne, IN

Russel Davison
Brandon High School
Brandon, FL

Christine K. Deyo
Rochester Adams High School
Rochester Hills, MI

Jim Doller
Fox Lane High School
Bedford, NY

Jessica Downing
Esparto High School
Esparto, CA

Douglas Fackelman
Brighton High School
Brighton, CO

Rick Forrest
Rochester High School
Rochester Hills, MI

Mark Freeman
Blacksburg High School
Blacksburg, VA

Jonathan Gillis
Enloe High School
Raleigh, NC

Karen Gruner
Holton Arms School
Bethesda, MD

Larry Harrison
DuPont Manual High School
Louisville, KY

Alan Haught
Weaver High School
Hartford, CT

Steven Iona
Horizon High School
Thornton, CO

Phil Jowell
Oak Ridge High School
Conroe, TX

Deborah Knight
Windsor Forest High School
Savannah, GA

Thomas Kobilarcik
Marist High School
Chicago, IL

Sheila Kolb
Plano Senior High School
Plano, TX

Todd Lindsay
Park Hill High School
Kansas City, MO

Malinda Mann
South Putnam High School
Greencastle, IN

Steve Martin
Maricopa High School
Maricopa, AZ

Nancy McGrory
North Quincy High School
N. Quincy, MA

David Morton
Mountain Valley High School
Rumford, ME

Charles Muller
Highland Park High School
Highland Park, NJ

Fred Muller
Mercy High School
Burlingame, CA

Vivian O'Brien
Plymouth Regional High School
Plymouth, NH

Robin Parkinson
Northridge High School
Layton, UT

Donald Perry
Newport High School
Bellevue, WA

Francis Poodry
Lincoln High School
Philadelphia, PA

John Potts
Custer County District High School
Miles City, MT

Doug Rich
Fox Lane High School
Bedford, NY

John Roeder
The Calhoun School
New York, NY

Consuelo Rogers
Maryknoll Schools
Honolulu, HI

Lee Rossmaessler, Ph.D
Mott Middle College High School
Flint, MI

John Rowe
Hughes Alternative Center
Cincinnati, OH

Rebecca Bonner Sanders
South Brunswick High School
Monmouth Junction, NJ

David Schlipp
Narbonne High School
Harbor City, CA

Eric Shackelford
Notre Dame High School
Sherman Oaks, CA

Robert Sorensen
Springville-Griffith Institute and
Central School
Springville, NY

Teresa Stalions
Crittenden County High School
Marion, KY

Roberta Tanner
Loveland High School
Loveland, CO

Anthony Umelo
Anacostia Sr. High School
Washington, D.C.

Judy Vondruska
Mitchell High School
Mitchell, SD

Deborah Waldron
Yorktown High School
Arlington, VA

Ken Wester
The Mississippi School for
Mathematics and Science
Columbus, MS

Susan Willis
Conroe High School
Conroe, TX

You can do physics. Here are the reasons why.

The following features make it that much easier to understand the physics principles you will be studying. Using all these features together will help you actually learn about this subject and see how it works for you everyday, everywhere. Look for all these features in each chapter of Active Physics.

② Challenge

This feature presents the problem you will soon be expected to solve, or the tasks you are expected to complete using the knowledge you gain in the chapter.

③ Criteria

Before the chapter begins you will learn exactly how you will be graded. Working with your classmates, you will even help determine the criteria by which your work will be evaluated.

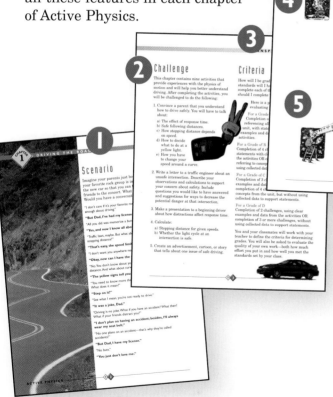

④ What Do You Think?

What do you already know? This unique feature encourages you to explore and discuss the ideas you have on a topic before you begin studying it.

⑤ For You to Do

In Active Physics you learn by doing. Activities encourage you to work through problems by yourself, in small groups, or with the whole class.

① Scenario

Each unit begins with a realistic event or situation you might actually have experienced, or can imagine yourself participating in at home, in school, or in your community.

⑥ Physics Talk

When you come across a physics term or equation in the chapter that you may not be familiar with, turn to this feature for a useful, easy-to-understand explanation.

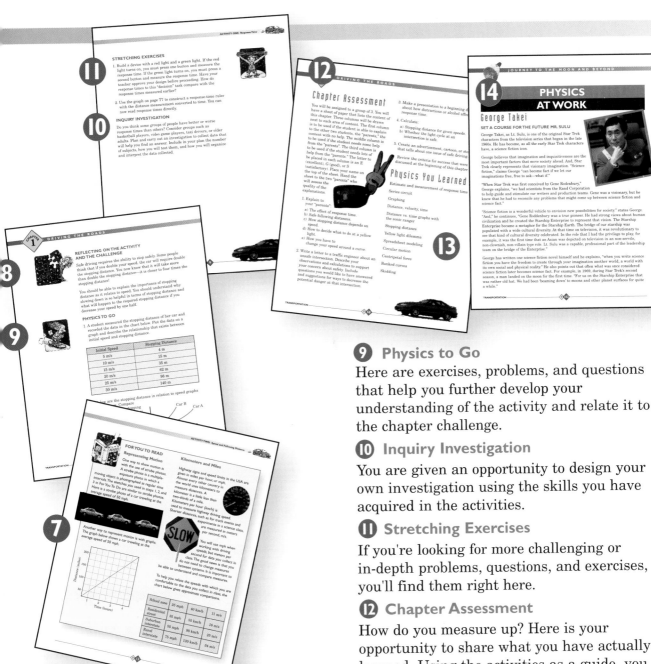

7 For You to Read

In this feature you will find additional insight, or perhaps an interesting new perspective into the topic of the activity.

8 Reflecting on the Activity and the Challenge

Each activity helps prepare you to be successful in the chapter challenge. This feature helps you relate this activity to the larger challenge. It's another piece of the chapter jigsaw puzzle.

9 Physics to Go

Here are exercises, problems, and questions that help you further develop your understanding of the activity and relate it to the chapter challenge.

10 Inquiry Investigation

You are given an opportunity to design your own investigation using the skills you have acquired in the activities.

11 Stretching Exercises

If you're looking for more challenging or in-depth problems, questions, and exercises, you'll find them right here.

12 Chapter Assessment

How do you measure up? Here is your opportunity to share what you have actually learned. Using the activities as a guide, you can now complete the challenge you were presented at the beginning of the chapter.

13 Physics You Learned

This lists the physics terms, principles, and skills you have just learned in the chapter.

14 Physics at Work

Using real people in real jobs, this feature demonstrates how the principles you are learning are being applied everyday, everywhere. It shows that people who use physics can make a difference.

Imagine meeting someone who never heard of your favorite movie or music group! Now imagine how enriched they would be if they could enjoy that movie or music the way you do.

Active Physics came about as a result of a similar frustration. The usual physics course has so much math and so much reading that many students miss the beauty, the excitement, and the usefulness of physics. Many more students simply refuse to take the course. Active Physics began when a group of physicists and physics teachers wondered how to pass on their enjoyment of physics to high school students.

Physics should be experienced and make sense to you. Each chapter of Active Physics begins with a challenge—develop a sport that can be played on the Moon; build a home for people with a housing crisis; pursuade your parents to lend you the family car; and so on. These are tough challenges, but you will learn the physics that will allow you to be successful at every one.

Part of your education is to learn to trust yourself and to question others. When someone tells you something, can they answer your questions: "How do you know? Why should I believe you? and Why should I care?" After Active Physics, when you describe why seatbelts are important, or why loud music can be hazardous, or why communication with extraterrestrials is difficult, and someone asks, "How do you know?" your answer will be, "I know because I did an experiment."

Only a small number of high school students study physics. You are already a part of this select group. Physics awaits your discovery. Enjoy the journey.

Arthur Eisenkraft

CHAPTER
1

DRIVING THE ROADS

Scenario

Imagine your parents just bought a new car and your favorite rock group is in town. You ask to use the new car so that you can take some of your friends to the concert. What would your parents say? Would you have a conversation like the following?

"I don't care if it's your favorite rock group. You don't know enough about driving."

"But Dad, I've had my license two whole months!"

"All you did was memorize a bunch of facts to get your license."

"Yes, and now I know all about the law."

"Traffic laws, maybe. But what about natural laws—speed and stopping distance?"

"That's easy, the speed limits are all posted."

"I don't want you anywhere near the speed limit."

"Okay, now can I have the car?"

"No. You don't know about your response time and following distance. And what about curves; when should you slow down?"

"The yellow signs tell you what to do on the curves."

"You need to know more than that. What about a yellow light? What does it mean?"

"Step on it?"

"See what I mean, you're not ready to drive."

"It was a joke, Dad."

"Driving is no joke. What if you have an accident? What then? What if your friends distract you?"

"I don't plan on having an accident; besides, I'll always wear my seat belt."

"No one plans on an accident—that's why they're called accidents!"

"But Dad, I have my license."

"No buts."

"You just don't love me."

Challenge

This chapter contains nine activities that provide experiences with the physics of motion and will help you better understand driving. After completing the activities, you will be challenged to do the following:

1. Convince a parent that you understand how to drive safely. You will have to talk about:
   a) The effect of response time.
   b) Safe following distances.
   c) How stopping distance depends on speed.
   d) How to decide what to do at a yellow light.
   e) How you have to change your speed around a curve.

2. Write a letter to a traffic engineer about an unsafe intersection. Describe your observations and calculations to support your concern about safety. Include questions you would like to have answered and suggestions for ways to decrease the potential danger at that intersection.

3. Make a presentation to a beginning driver about how distractions affect response time.

4. Calculate:
   a) Stopping distance for given speeds.
   b) Whether the light cycle at an intersection is safe.

5. Create an advertisement, cartoon, or story that tells about one issue of safe driving.

Criteria

How will I be graded? What quality standards will I have to meet to successfully complete each of the challenges? How many should I complete to receive an "A?"

Here is a possible rubric (criteria), for evaluating your success.

For a Grade of A
Completion of all 5 challenges, referencing all concepts presented in unit, with statements supported by clear examples and data collected from the activities.

For a Grade of B
Completion of 4 challenges, supporting all statements with clear examples and data from the activities OR completion of all 5 challenges, referring to concepts from unit, but without using collected data to support statements.

For a Grade of C
Completion of 3 challenges, using clear examples and data from the activities OR completion of 4 challenges, referring to concepts from the unit, but without using collected data to support statements.

For a Grade of D
Completion of 2 challenges, using clear examples and data from the activities OR completion of 3 or more challenges, without using collected data to support statements.

You and your classmates will work with your teacher to define the criteria for determining grades. You will also be asked to evaluate the quality of your own work—both how much effort you put in and how well you met the standards set by your class.

Activity One

Response Time

WHAT DO YOU THINK?

Many deaths that occur on the highway are drivers and passengers in vehicles that did not cause the accident. The driver was not able to respond in time to avoid becoming a statistic.

• **How long would it take you to respond to an emergency?**

Record your ideas about these questions in your *Active Physics log*. Be prepared to discuss your responses with your small group and the class.

FOR YOU TO DO

1. To stop a car, you must move your foot from the gas pedal to the brake pedal. Try moving your right foot between imaginary pedals.

a) Estimate how long it takes to move your foot between the imaginary pedals. Record your estimate.

2. The first step in stopping a car happens even before you move your foot to the brake. It takes time to see or hear something that tells you to move your foot. Test this by having a friend stand behind you and clap. When you hear the sound, move your foot between imaginary pedals.

a) Estimate how long it took you to respond to the loud noise. Record your estimate.

3. Create a simple electric circuit to test your response time. Your group will need a battery in a clip, two switches, a flashlight bulb in a socket, and connecting wires. Connect the wires from one terminal of the battery to the first switch, then to the second switch, to the light bulb, and back to the battery.

 **Have your teacher approve your circuit before proceeding to step 4.**

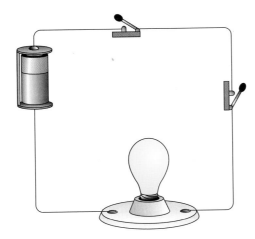

4. Close one switch while the other is open. Close the other switch. Take turns turning the light off and on with each person operating only one switch.

a) Record what happens in each case.

5. Try to keep the light on for exactly one second, then five seconds. You can estimate one second by saying "one thousand one."

a) How quickly do you think you can turn the light off after your partner turns it on? The time the bulb is lit is your response time. Record an estimate of your response time in your log.

6. Find your response time using the electric circuit.

✎a) How could you improve the accuracy of the measure?

✎b) How would repeating the investigation improve the accuracy?

7. Test your response time with the other equipment set up in your classroom. Use a standard reaction time meter, such as one used in driver education. You will need to follow the directions for the model available in your class.

✎a) Record your response time.

8. Use two stopwatches. One person starts both stopwatches at the same time, and hands one to her lab partner. When the first person stops her watch, the lab partner stops his. The difference in the two times is the response time.

✎a) Record your response time.

9. Use a centimeter ruler. Hold the centimeter ruler at the top, between thumb and forefinger, with zero at the bottom. Your partner places thumb and forefinger at the lower end, but does not touch the ruler. Drop the ruler. Your partner must stop the ruler from falling by closing thumb and forefinger.

✎a) The position of your partner's fingers marks the distance the ruler fell while her nervous system was responding. Record the distance in your log.

✎b) The graph at the top of page T7 shows the relationship between the distance the ruler fell and the time it took to stop it. Use the graph to find and record your response time.

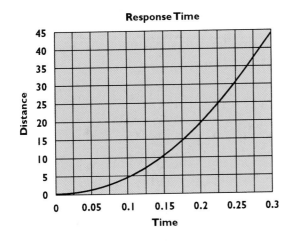

Response Time

10. Compare the measures of your response obtained from each strategy.

a) Explain why they were not all the same.

b) What measure do you think best reports your response time? Why?

11. Compare the measures you obtained with those of other students.

a) Record the results for the fastest, slowest, and average response times.

b) Why do you think response times vary for people of the same age? Discuss this with your group and then record your answer.

REFLECTING ON THE ACTIVITY AND THE CHALLENGE

The amount of time a person requires before they can act has a direct impact on their driving. It takes time to notice a situation and more time to respond. A person who requires a second to respond to what they see or hear is more likely to have an accident than someone who responds in half a second. One part of your challenge is to explain the effect of response time on driving.

PHYSICS TO GO

1. Test the response time of some of your friends and family with the centimeter ruler. Bring in the results from at least three people of various ages.

2. How do the values you found in question 1 compare with those you obtained in class? What do you think explains the difference, if any?

3. Take a dollar bill and fold it in half lengthwise. Have someone try to catch the dollar bill between his or her *forefinger and middle* finger. Most people will fail this task.

    a) Explain why it is so difficult to catch the dollar bill.
    b) Repeat the dollar bill test, letting them catch it with their thumb and forefinger.
    c) Explain why catching it with thumb and forefinger may have been easier. Try to include numbers in your answer such as length of the dollar, time for dollar to fall, and average response time.

4. Does a race car driver need a better response time than someone driving around a school? Explain your answer, giving examples of the dangers each person encounters.

5. Apply what you learned from this activity to describe how knowing your own response time can help you be a safer driver. You will use this in meeting the challenge at the end of the chapter.

STRETCHING EXERCISES

1. Build a device with a red light and a green light. If the red light turns on, you must press one button and measure the response time. If the green light turns on, you must press a second button and measure the response time. Have your teacher approve your design before proceeding. How do response times to this "decision" task compare with the response times measured earlier?

2. Use the graph on page T7 to construct a response-time ruler with the distance measurement converted to time. You can now read response times directly.

INQUIRY INVESTIGATION

Do you think some groups of people have better or worse response times than others? Consider groups such as basketball players, video game players, taxi drivers, or older adults. Plan and carry out an investigation to collect data that will help you find an answer. Include in your plan the number of subjects, how you will test them, and how you will organize and interpret the data collected.

Activity Two

Speed and Following Distance

WHAT DO YOU THINK?

In a rear-end collision, the driver of the car in back is always found at fault.

- **What is a safe distance between your car and the car in front of you?**
- **How do you decide?**

Record your ideas about these questions in your *Active Physics log*. Be prepared to discuss your responses with your small group and the class.

FOR YOU TO DO

1. A strobe photo is a multiple-exposure photo in which a moving object is photographed at regular time intervals. The strobe photo below shows a car traveling at 30 mph.

   ✎ a) Copy the sketch in your log.

2. Think about the difference between the motion of a car traveling at 30 mph and one traveling at 45 mph.

   ✎ a) Draw a sketch of a strobe photo, similar to the one above, of a car traveling at 45 mph.

b) Are the cars the same distance apart? Were they farther apart or closer together than at 30 mph?

c) Draw a sketch for a car traveling at 60 mph. Describe how you decided how far apart to place the cars.

3. The following sketch shows a car traveling at different speeds.

a) Copy the sketch in your log. Mark where the car is traveling fast, where it is traveling slow, and where it is traveling at a constant speed. How did you know?

4. A sonic ranger connected to a computer will produce a graph that shows an object's motion. Use the sonic ranger setup to obtain the following graphs to print or sketch in your log.

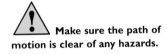 **Make sure the path of motion is clear of any hazards.**

a) Sketch a graph of a person walking toward the sonic ranger at a normal speed.

b) Sketch a graph of a person walking away from the sonic ranger at a normal speed.

c) Sketch a graph of a person walking both directions at a very slow speed.

d) Sketch a graph of a person walking both directions at a fast speed.

5. Predict what the graph will look like if you walk toward the system at a slow speed and away at a fast speed. Test your prediction.

a) Record your prediction in your log.

b) Based on your measurements, how accurate was your prediction?

6. Repeat any of the motions in steps 4 or 5 for a more thorough analysis.

✎ a) From your graph, determine the total distance you walked.

✎ b) How long did it take to walk that distance?

✎ c) Divide the distance you walked by the time it took. This is your average speed in meters per second (m/s).

PHYSICS TALK

Speed

The relationship between speed, distance, and time can be written as:

$$\text{Speed} = \frac{\text{Distance}}{\text{Time}}$$

If your speed is changing, this gives your average speed.

Examples

You drive 400 miles in 8 hours. What is your average speed?

$$\text{Speed} = \frac{\text{Distance}}{\text{Time}}$$

$$= \frac{400 \text{ miles}}{8 \text{ hours}}$$

$$= 50 \text{ miles per hour}$$

Your average speed is 50 miles per hour. This does not tell the fastest you went, nor the slowest.

If you are going 35 mph (16 m/s) and your reaction time is 0.2 s, the distance you travel during your reaction time is

$$\text{Distance} = \text{Speed} \times \text{Time}$$

$$d = 16 \text{ m/s} \times 0.2 \text{ s}$$

$$= 3.2 \text{ m}$$

FOR YOU TO READ

Representing Motion

One way to show motion is with the use of strobe photos. A strobe photo is a multiple-exposure photo in which a moving object is photographed at regular time intervals. The sketches you used in steps 1, 2, and 3 in For You To Do are similar to strobe photos. Here is a strobe photo of a car traveling at the average speed of 50 mph.

Another way to represent motion is with graphs. The graph below shows a car traveling at the average speed of 50 mph.

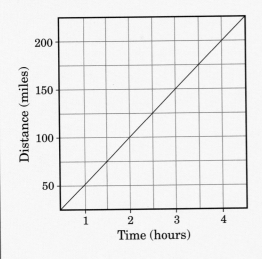

Kilometers and Miles

Highway signs and speed limits in the USA are given in miles per hour, or mph. Almost every other country in the world uses kilometers to measure distances. A kilometer is a little less than two-thirds of a mile. Kilometers per hour (km/h) is used to measure highway driving speed. Shorter distances, such as for track events and experiments in a science class, are measured in meters per second, m/s.

You will use mph when working with driving speeds, but meters per second for data you collect in class. The good news is that you do not need to change measures between systems. It is important to be able to understand and compare measures.

To help you relate the speeds with which you are comfortable to the data you collect in class, the chart below gives *approximate* comparisons.

School zone	25 mph	40 km/h	11 m/s
Residential street	35 mph	55 km/h	16 m/s
Suburban interstate	55 mph	90 km/h	25 m/s
Rural interstate	75 mph	120 km/h	34 m/s

REFLECTING ON THE ACTIVITY AND THE CHALLENGE

You know that response time has a direct impact on your driving and the possibility of being involved in a car accident. In this activity you observed what happens to the car while the driver responds before applying the brake. The car continues moving. The slower a person's response time, the greater the distance the car moves before stopping.

You now know how reaction time and speed affect the distance to stop. You should be able to make a good argument about tailgating as part of the chapter challenge.

PHYSICS TO GO

1. Describe the motion of each car moving to the right. The strobe pictures were taken every 3 s (seconds).

   a)
   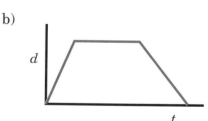

   b)
   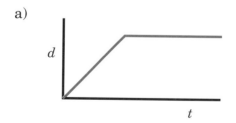

2. Sketch strobe pictures of the following.

   a) A car starting at rest and reaching a final constant speed.
   b) A car traveling at a constant speed then coming to a stop.

3. For each graph below, describe the motion of the car:

   a)

   b)

   c)

   d)
   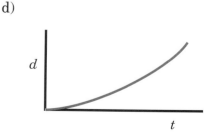

4. A race car driver travels at 110 m/s (that's almost 250 mph) for 20 s. How far has the driver traveled?

5. A salesperson drove the 215 miles from New York City to Washington, DC, in $4\frac{1}{2}$ hours.

   a) What was her average speed?
   b) How fast was she going when she passed through Baltimore?

6. If you planned to bike to a park that was 5 miles away, what average speed would you have to keep up to arrive in 2 hours?

7. Use your average response time from Activity 1 to answer the following:

   a) How far does your car travel in meters during your response time if you are moving at 55 mph (25 m/s)?
   b) How far does your car travel during your response time if you are moving at 35 mph (16 m/s)? How does the distance compare with the distance at 55 mph?
   c) Suppose you are very tired and your response time is doubled. How far would you travel at 55 mph during your response time?

8. According to traffic experts, the proper following distance you should leave between your car and the vehicle in front of you is two seconds. As the vehicle in front of you passes a fixed point, say to yourself "one thousand one, one thousand two." Your car should reach the point as you complete the phrase. How can the experts be sure? Isn't two seconds a measure of time? Will two seconds be safe on the interstate highway?

9. You calculated the distance your car would move during your response time. Use that information to determine a safe following distance at:

   a) 25 mph
   b) 55 mph
   c) 75 mph

10. Apply what you learned in this activity to write a convincing argument that describes why following a car too closely (tailgating) is dangerous. Include the factors you would use to decide how close counts as "tailgating."

STRETCHING EXERCISES

Measure a distance of about 100 m. You can use a football field or get a long tape or trundle wheel to measure a similar distance. You also need a watch capable of measuring seconds. Determine your average speed traveling that distance for each of the following:

    a) a slow walk

    b) a fast walk

    c) running

    d) on a bicycle

    e) a method of your choice

Activity Three
Stopping Your Car

WHAT DO YOU THINK?

In 1995, only 14% of speed-related traffic deaths happened on interstate highways. Imagine you are driving at the speed limit, and you suddenly see a moose crossing the road ahead of you.

- **Will you be able to stop in time to avoid hitting the moose?**
- **What are all the factors that determine how soon you will be able to stop the car?**

Record your ideas about these questions in your *Active Physics log*. Be prepared to discuss your responses with your small group and the class.

FOR YOU TO DO

1. Start the car moving by letting it roll down a ramp. You can control its speed by starting it at various distances up the ramp, or by changing the slope of the ramp.

2. Use a photogate or sonic ranger to measure the car's speed at the moment it gets to the bottom of the ramp. This is the speed the car is traveling at the moment the stopping process begins. This is called the **initial speed**.

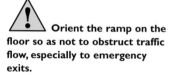 Orient the ramp on the floor so as not to obstruct traffic flow, especially to emergency exits.

If you are setting the ramp up on the table, provide some means to contain the cart and prevent it from flying from the table.

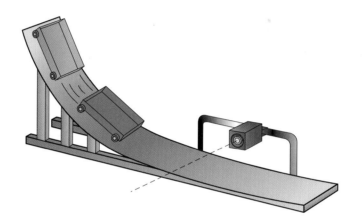

3. Find the distance the car travels from the bottom of the ramp to the point where it stops. This is the **stopping distance**.

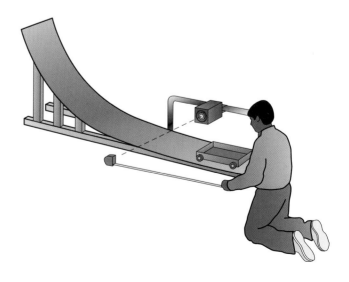

4. Do at least 10 trials with the car going at different speeds and measure the corresponding stopping distances.

   a) Record your data in a chart like the one below.

Initial Speed (m/s)	Distance Traveled (m)

5. One way to display data is on a graph. In this activity you are interested in seeing how the stopping distance relates to the initial speed. Place the initial speed on the horizontal axis and the stopping distance on the vertical axis.

   a) Plot a graph of your data in your log.
   b) How does the stopping distance change with initial speed?
   c) What kind of relationship does your graph show?

6. Select two values of speed from your graph, with one value just double the other. When the speed of the car doubles, what happens to the stopping distance?

   a) What is the effect of doubling speed on distance traveled during response time? (Refer to Activity 2)
   b) What is the effect of doubling speed on distance traveled during stopping?

7. Compare two stopping distances for which the second speed is three times as fast.

   a) What is the effect of tripling the speed on the distance traveled during stopping?
   b) Predict how going four times as fast will affect stopping distance.

REFLECTING ON THE ACTIVITY AND THE CHALLENGE

Safe driving requires the ability to stop safely. Some people think that if you double your speed, the car will require double the stopping distance. You now know that it will take more than double the stopping distance—it is closer to four times the stopping distance!

You should be able to explain the importance of stopping distance as it relates to speed. You should understand why slowing down is so helpful in terms of stopping distance and what will happen to the required stopping distance if you decrease your speed by one half.

PHYSICS TO GO

1. A student measured the stopping distance of her car and recorded the data in the chart below. Plot the data on a graph and describe the relationship that exists between initial speed and stopping distance.

Initial Speed	Stopping Distance
5 m/s	4 m
10 m/s	15 m
15 m/s	35 m
20 m/s	62 m
25 m/s	98 m
30 m/s	140 m

2. Below are the stopping distance in relation to speed graphs for two cars. Compare qualitatively the stopping distances when each car is going at a slow speed and then again at a higher speed. Which car is safer? Why?

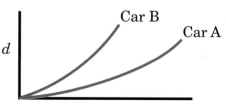

3. A car is able to stop in 20 m when traveling at 30 mph. How much distance will it require to stop when traveling at:

   a) 15 mph? (half of 30 mph)
   b) 60 mph? (twice 30 mph)
   c) 45 mph? (three times 15 mph)
   d) 75 mph? (five times 15 mph)

4. A car traveling at 10 m/s requires a stopping distance of 30 m. If the driver requires 0.9 s response time, what additional distance will the car travel before stopping?

5. Consult the information for the 1998 Corvette Convertible found on page T56 of this book. This shows the stopping distance from *Road & Track* magazine. How far would you expect this car to travel until coming to rest when brakes are applied at a speed of 30 mph?

6. Use the information on page T55. Find the braking distances for 50 mph and 25 mph. Create a graph using the different braking distances. Plot the speeds on the horizontal axis and the stopping distances on the vertical axis.

7. Does the braking information on page T55 include the driver's response time? Who should let the consumer know about this—the information sheet or a driver training manual?

8. Apply what you learned from this activity to write a statement explaining the factors that affect stopping distance. What do you now know about stopping that will make you a safer driver?

Activity Four
Putting It All Together

WHAT DO YOU THINK?

While enjoying good music, a person's response time is slower.

- **What is the effect of a slowed response time?**
- **What could you do to improve your response time?**

Record your ideas about these questions in your *Active Physics log*. Be prepared to discuss your responses with your small group and the class.

FOR YOU TO DO

Design Your Own Investigation

1. Think about the conditions you would encounter when driving in your area.

   a) Make a list of 10 things that might slow down your response time. For example, listening to a car stereo may be such a distraction.

2. In this activity you will investigate the effect of distractions on response time. As a conclusion, you will relate your results to safe driving.

   a) Choose one of the things that you listed in step 1 to investigate. Record it in your log in the form of a question.

3. Follow your teacher's guidelines for using time, space, and materials as you carry out the investigation and prepare your report and conclusions.

   a) Make a list of materials you will need, the procedure you will use, and how you will organize and report the data that you collect.

   b) After your teacher has approved your procedure, carry out your investigation.

REFLECTING ON THE ACTIVITY AND THE CHALLENGE

Teenagers often have a very good response time. You now know that drinking, listening to loud music, and even eating french fries while you drive can slow down your response time.

Based on this activity, you may have new ideas about other activities or behaviors that could slow your response time. Write these in your log.

PHYSICS TO GO

1. Write a paragraph about the factors that you must consider when calculating the distance a car travels, from the instant you see danger to finally stopping the car.

2. Many driver education manuals describe stopping in the following way: IDENTIFY the problem; PREDICT what may happen; DECIDE what to do; and EXECUTE your decision. Does this description exaggerate the process of stopping?

3. One of your friends tells you, "I always tailgate. I never get into an accident because I pay attention and I'm quick!" What can you say to your friend to convince him that this is not smart driving?

TRANSPORTATION

4. Alcohol-related crashes and injuries cost society $46 billion each year in lost income, medical bills, property damage, and other costs. Knowing this, why do you think people still drive after drinking?

5. Why do you think it is against the law to drive while under the influence of alcohol?

6. Apply what you learned from this activity to explain to your parents why it is not safe to drive while talking on a car phone. How could you use this information to improve your argument for the opening challenge?

STRETCHING EXERCISES

Driving Simulation

It is often stated that when following a car on a highway, you should allow a minimum of one car length of space for each 10 mph of speed.

- Would you do this?
- How far behind a car do you usually follow?
- If the driver in front of you suddenly braked, at that distance would you have enough room to stop?
- Do you think that having one car length of space for each 10 mph is enough?

Ask your teacher for the **Driving Simulation** computer game so you can test that theory. In the game, two cars are cruising at the same steady speed on a two-lane road. You are driving the second car. Suddenly you see the brake lights on the lead car. Your response time determines your fate. When driving, you are usually preoccupied and don't expect the car in front of you to stop. Therefore, this game is designed to take your mind off the lead car.

Note: Do not try to anticipate or ready yourself for braking. The idea is to get an accurate measure of your braking response time, not to beat the clock.

Directions

1. Open the spreadsheet DRIVESIM.XLS. Click on the "start" button for the simulation to begin.

2. When you see the red stoplight, quickly move the mouse to the brake button and click. Your response time will be displayed.

3. Read the manufacturer's recommendations for the stopping distance of a car at 55 mph. The lead car will stop in this distance. Your car will stop in this distance plus the distance you traveled before you reacted to the brake lights. That extra distance can be calculated from this equation:

   extra distance = speed × response time.

4. If you are closer to the lead car than this extra distance, you will have an accident. To find out the necessary distance, follow these steps:

   Click on the tab at the bottom of the spreadsheet labeled "Calculations."

   Measure the length of an average car or use the manufacturer's specifications. Enter that number in the box labeled "Car Lengths."

   Enter recommended trailing distance in "Car Lengths."

   Calculate your extra braking distance.

   Enter your speed in mph and your response time in the boxes.

5. Compare your extra distance with the recommended following distance. Will this following distance cause an accident?

6. Discuss the safety of the original distance assumption about allowing one car length for every 10 mph.

Note: To enter a number on the spreadsheet, click in the box, type the number (do not include units or commas) and press <Enter>. If you get the message "Locked cells cannot be changed" it means that you did not click in the proper box. Try again.

Activity Five

Intersections with a Yellow Light

WHAT DO YOU THINK?

Some traffic lights stay yellow for 3 seconds. Others stay yellow for 6 seconds.

• **If all traffic lights stayed yellow the same amount of time, how would this affect drivers' decisions at intersections?**

Take a few minutes to write your ideas in your log. Discuss your response with your small group and see if you agree or disagree. Be prepared to discuss your responses with your small group and the class.

FOR YOU TO DO

1. Watch the video of an intersection, carefully noting what happens when the light turns yellow.

   a) Are there cars that you think should have stopped?

   b) Were there cars that stopped, but you think should have continued through the intersection?

2. Watch the video a second time, this time paying attention to the position of the cars at the moment the light turns yellow.

   a) Can you identify a "cutoff" point for a car to make it through the intersection before the light turns red?

3. The diagram below shows the position of three cars at the moment a light turns yellow. Car A is able to make it through the intersection before the light turns red. It is in the GO Zone. Car C may not be able to make it through the yellow light. The light may turn red before car C gets to the intersection.

   a) Will car B be able to make it through the yellow light?
   b) Is car B in the GO Zone?
   c) Would any car closer to the intersection than car A be in the GO Zone?
   d) Is car C in the GO Zone?

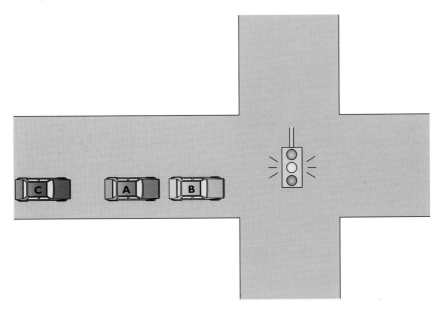

4. In the next diagram of an intersection car D is able to come to a safe stop. This car is in the STOP Zone. Car F is closer to the intersection than car D. If the driver of this car tries to stop the car, he may not be able to stop in such a short distance.

   a) Is car E in the STOP Zone? Why or why not?

   b) Is car F in the STOP Zone? Why or why not?

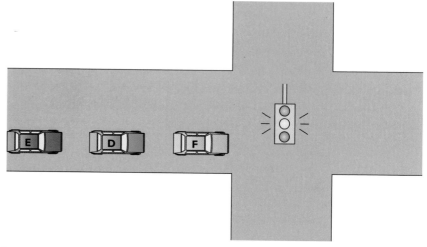

   c) Sketch the STOP Zone and GO Zone for the intersection in the diagrams. Place cars A to F in the appropriate zones.

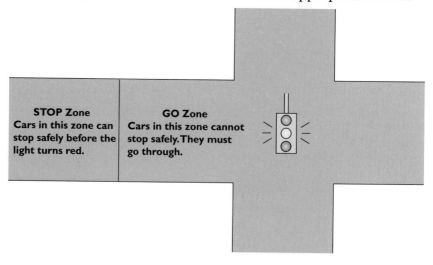

5. In order to study the yellow light problem, transportation engineers use a computer simulation to model how various factors affect the GO Zone and the STOP Zone. In the model on the following page there are five input variables that can affect the two output variables.

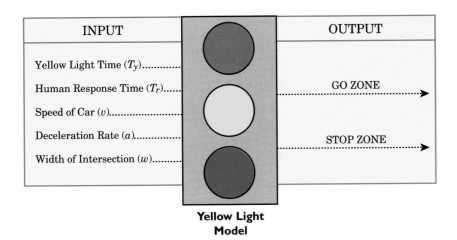

INPUT		OUTPUT
Yellow Light Time (T_y)............		
Human Response Time (T_r)......		GO ZONE
Speed of Car (v)........................		
Deceleration Rate (a)..............		STOP ZONE
Width of Intersection (w)..........		

Yellow Light Model

a) List the five variables shown in the model.

b) You will first study how the variables affect the GO Zone. Copy the chart below in your log.

Variable	Change		Predicted Effect of Change on GO Zone	Actual Effect of Change on GO Zone
T_y	Yellow Light Time	increase T_y		
		decrease T_y		
T_r	Response Time	increase T_r		
		decrease T_r		
v	Speed Limit	increase v		
		decrease v		
a	Deceleration Rate	increase a		
		decrease a		
w	Width of Intersection	increase w		
		decrease w		

c) Predict how increasing or decreasing each variable affects the size of the GO Zone. Remember to consider one variable at a time; the other four variables will stay constant. For example, if the time the light is yellow increases from 3 s to 3.5 s, how will the boundaries and size of the GO Zone change? Will the zone increase or decrease? Record your predictions.

6. Look at the copies of the spreadsheets shown below.

   a) What is the distance of the GO Zone if the yellow light is 3 s?
   b) What happens to the GO Zone when the yellow light time is increased to 3.5 s?
   c) Does this make sense to you? Would increasing the yellow light allow you to get through the intersection from a greater distance away? Explain your answer in your log.
   d) Record the actual effect of the yellow light time in your log.

	A	B	C	D	E	F	G
1	**INPUT VARIABLES**					**OUTPUT**	
2	Yellow Light Time (T_y)	3	seconds		53	meters	Go Zone
3	Human Response Time (T_r)	1	seconds	YELLOW	60	meters	Stop Zone
4	Speed of car (v)	20	m/s	LIGHT			
5	Deceleration rate (a)	5	m/s/s	MODEL			
6	Width of Intersection (w)	7	meters				
7							
8							
9							

	A	B	C	D	E	F	G
1	**INPUT VARIABLES**						
2						**OUTPUT**	
3	Yellow Light Time (T_y)	3.5	seconds				
4	Human Response Time (T_r)	1	seconds	YELLOW	63	meters	Go Zone
5	Speed of car (v)	20	m/s	LIGHT	60	meters	Stop Zone
6	Deceleration rate (a)	5	m/s/s	MODEL			
7	Width of Intersection (w)	7	meters				
8							
9							

7. Use the computer investigation to obtain quantitative data, or numbers, you can use to test your predictions. Remember to change only one variable at a time. For each variable you investigate, record the following.

a) Did the effect of the change of the variable make sense to you? Explain.

b) Record the actual effect of changing each variable in your log. How did the actual effect compare with your prediction?

8. Try to determine how the GO Zone is calculated from the results of your spreadsheet investigation.

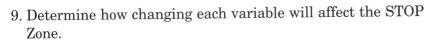

E	F OUTPUT	G
	meters	Go Zone
=(B5*B3)–B7	meters	Stop Zone
=(B5*B4)+(B5^2)/(2*B6)		

a) Describe how the spreadsheet computes the GO Zone by clicking on the cell which gives the GO Zone value. Look at the formula bar and convert this notation to an equation. Record this equation in your journal.

b) Compare your relationship with your group and explain why the yellow light time, velocity, and the width of the intersection appear in the equation for the GO Zone.

c) Why do the response time and deceleration rate not appear in the equation?

9. Determine how changing each variable will affect the STOP Zone.

a) Record your predictions in a chart similar to the one you used for the GO Zone.

b) Use the spreadsheet investigation to find the actual effect of each variable on the STOP Zone. Record the effect in your chart.

c) Compare your prediction with the actual effect. Do your results make sense to you? Explain.

10. Determine how the STOP Zone is calculated from the results of your spreadsheet investigation.

a) Describe how the spreadsheet computes the STOP Zone by clicking on the cell which gives the STOP Zone value. Look at the formula bar and convert this notation to an equation. Record this equation in your journal.

b) Compare your relationship with your group and explain why the yellow light time and the width of the intersection do not appear in the equation for the STOP Zone.

c) Why do the response time, velocity, and deceleration rate appear in the equation?

REFLECTING ON THE ACTIVITY AND THE CHALLENGE

In earlier investigations, you learned that a car travels a certain distance while you are moving at a constant velocity and deciding to stop. You also learned that your car travels a certain distance after the brakes have been applied.

In this activity you learned that deciding whether you have enough distance to stop when you see a yellow light is not a simple decision. It requires a judgment of the distance to the intersection, the width of the intersection, and how much time it will take you to get there at the speed you are traveling.

You now know which factors affect the GO Zone and which affect the STOP Zone. You also know how these zones may change if your response time is poorer or if your deceleration rate is being affected by bad weather or road conditions. Part of the chapter challenge is to explain these factors and your driving response based on your investigations and conclusions.

PHYSICS TO GO

1. An Active Physics student group is studying an intersection. The width of the intersection is measured by pacing and is found to be approximately 15 m wide. The yellow light time for the intersection is 4 s. The speed limit on this road is 30 miles per hour (approximately 15 m/s). The speed of the car decreases by 5 m/s every second during deceleration. Assume that people driving have a response time of 1.0 s.

   a) Calculate the GO Zone using the math equation on the computer spreadsheet. Use a calculator. To guide you, the first two steps are given.

   GO Zone = velocity × yellow light time − width of intersection
   $$GZ = vt_y - w$$
   $$GZ = (15 \text{ m/s})(4 \text{ s}) - 15 \text{ m}$$
   $$GZ = \rule{3cm}{0.4pt}$$

b) Calculate the STOP Zone using the math equation on the computer spreadsheet. Use a calculator to help you.

STOP Zone = velocity × response time + velocity²/2 × deceleration rate

$SZ = vt + v^2/2a$

$SZ = $ ☐

c) Make a sketch of the intersection and label both the GO Zone and the STOP Zone. Include the dimensions of the intersection and each zone.

2. A person is listening to loud music while driving. Explain why the increase in response time caused by the music does not affect the GO Zone. Explain how it affects the STOP Zone.

3. A car has worn tires and bad brakes. How will this affect the GO Zone and the STOP Zone at a yellow light?

4. Some people disregard the 40 mph speed limit (20 m/s) and travel at 60 mph (30 m/s) on the road described in question 1. Calculate STOP and GO Zones at this speed. Write several sentences and sketch the intersection to inform these drivers of the danger of driving at 60 mph if the light turned yellow.

5. How would a decrease in the speed limit to 20 mph (about 10 m/s) affect the STOP and GO Zones in question 1? Use the spreadsheet or calculator to calculate both, then sketch the intersection, marking both zones.

6. Go out near your school and take measurements at an intersection that has a traffic light. Use the spreadsheet program or a calculator to calculate the STOP and GO Zones, then make a scale drawing of the intersection that includes both zones.

⚠ **Excercise extreme caution. Follow the safety procedures outlined by your teacher. It is recommended that this activity be carried out with co-operation of the local Police Department.**

7. Do you think it would be a good idea to paint lines at all intersections showing the boundaries of the STOP and GO Zones? Why or why not?

Activity Six
Yellow Light Dilemma and Dangerous Intersections

WHAT DO YOU THINK?

Almost 70% of the people killed by automobiles in New Mexico are pedestrians.

- **How could an intersection with a traffic light be dangerous?**
- **How could it be made safer?**

Record your ideas about these questions in your *Active Physics log*. Be prepared to discuss your responses with your small group and the class.

FOR YOU TO DO

1. Imagine that you are at intersection 1 shown below.

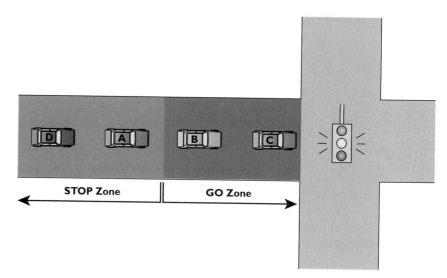

a) Would you "go" or "stop" if the light turned yellow when your car was in position A? in position B? in position C? in position D?

2. Imagine that you are at intersection 2 shown below.

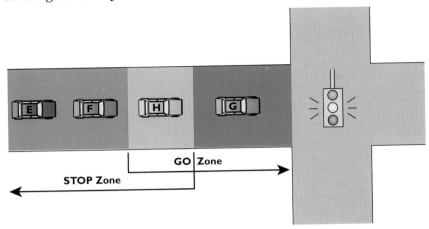

   a) Would you "go" or "stop" if the light turned yellow when your car was in position E? in position F? in position G? in position H?

3. Imagine you are at intersection 3 shown below.

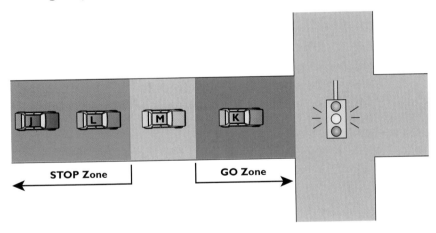

   a) Would you "go" or "stop" if the light turned yellow when your car was in position J? in position K? in position L? in position M?

4. Compare the GO Zone and the STOP Zone for intersections 1, 2, and 3.

   a) How are the intersections different?

   b) In intersection 2, if the light turned yellow when you were in the overlap between the GO Zone and the STOP Zone, what are your choices? Which choice(s) would be safe?

   c) In intersection 3, if the light turned yellow when you were in the space between the STOP Zone and the GO Zone, what are your choices? Which choice(s) would be safe?

   d) When both choices are safe, the space between the GO and STOP Zones is called the Overlap Zone. When neither choice is clearly safe, it is called the Dilemma Zone. Intersections with a Dilemma Zone are not safe. Which intersection has an Overlap Zone and which has a Dilemma Zone?

5. Use a computer spreadsheet program, very similar to the one you used in Activity 5. There is an additional OUTPUT that tells you whether the intersection is safe and has an Overlap Zone or is unsafe and has a Dilemma Zone. Use the spreadsheet to determine ways in which an unsafe intersection can be made into a safe intersection and vice versa.

   a) How does the spreadsheet figure out whether the intersection is safe? What is the relationship between the GO Zone and the STOP Zone at an unsafe intersection?

	A	B	C	D	E	F	G
1	**INPUT VARIABLES**					**OUTPUT**	
2							
3	Yellow Light Time (T_y)	3.7	seconds				
4	Human Response Time (T_r)	1.2	seconds	YELLOW	64	meters	Go Zone
5	Speed of Car (v)	20	m/s	LIGHT	64	meters	Stop Zone
6	Deceleration Rate (a)	5	m/s/s	MODEL	0	meters	Overlap Zone
7	Width of Intersection (w)	10	meters				Safe
8							
9							
10							
11	Yellow Light Time (T_y)	3.7	seconds				
12	Human Response Time (T_r)	1.2	seconds	YELLOW	101	meters	Go Zone
13	Speed of Car (v)	30	m/s	LIGHT	126	meters	Stop Zone
14	Deceleration Rate (a)	5	m/s/s	MODEL	–25	meters	Dilemma Zone
15	Width of Intersection (w)	10	meters				UNSAFE
16							

b) Use the sample spreadsheet shown. Is there an Overlap or Dilemma Zone at 20 m/s?

c) What happens to the GO Zone and the STOP Zone when the speed is increased to 30 m/s? Is there still an Overlap or Dilemma Zone?

d) Now lower the speed to 10 m/s (20 mph). Is the intersection now safer? Why or why not?

6. Continue your exploration by resetting the speed to its original value of 20 m/s. Adjust the yellow light time and determine its effect on the Dilemma and Overlap Zones.

a) Record the results of this investigation in your log.

7. What effect do human response time, deceleration rate, and width of the intersection have on the safety of the intersection? Conduct investigations with your spreadsheet.

a) Record the results in your log.

8. More than one variable change can eliminate a Dilemma Zone and replace it with an Overlap Zone.

a) Of the five variables, explain the ease or difficulty in changing each one to make the intersection safer. For example, why might you suggest changing the yellow light time rather than changing the width of the intersection?

9. The Yellow Light Problem is based on a simple model and only provides approximate calculations. It does not include other factors such as whether the road is flat or the length of your car.

a) How does the length of the car affect the model? Which outputs are affected by the length of your car?

REFLECTING ON THE ACTIVITY AND THE CHALLENGE

It appears from this activity that a traffic engineer has to be sure that an intersection has an overlap zone and not a dilemma zone. As you now know, any intersection can be made safer by slowing the speed limit or by lengthening the yellow light time. Occasionally a light is mounted at the intersection and its time is not adjusted but left at the manufacturer's default value. Accidents are more likely to occur at such an intersection because it may have a dilemma zone. Part of your chapter challenge is to write a letter to a traffic engineer about an unsafe intersection. If you complete question 5 in the Physics to Go, you have already completed this part of your challenge.

PHYSICS TO GO

1. Compute the GO Zones and STOP Zones for each intersection. Also determine if each intersection is safe and describe how you know.

   a) Yellow light time   3.0 s
      Response time   1.2 s
      Speed of car   20 m/s
      Deceleration rate   7 m/s/s
      Width of intersection   12 m

   b) Yellow light time   4.0 s
      Response time   1.2 s
      Speed of car   20 m/s
      Deceleration rate   7 m/s/s
      Width of intersection   8 m

   c) Yellow light time   3.0 s
      Response time   1.0 s
      Speed of car   20 m/s
      Deceleration rate   7 m/s/s
      Width of intersection   12 m

   d) Yellow light time   3.0s
      Response time   1.8 s
      Speed of car   20 m/s
      Deceleration rate   7 m/s/s
      Width of intersection   12 m

e) Yellow light time   3.5 s
    Response time   1.2 s
    Speed of car   15 m/s
    Deceleration rate   7 m/s/s
    Width of intersection   12 m

2. Another name for the Dilemma Zone could be the "You're in Big Trouble Zone." Can you think of a catchier phrase or name that will help you explain to your friends the problems in this unsafe zone?

3. The stopping distance of a car approaching a yellow light depends on response time and speed. Write a paragraph in your *Active Physics log* that applies all of this information to making a wise decision when in the Dilemma Zone.

4. Now that you know how the length of the yellow light time and other factors affect the safety of a traffic intersection, you are ready to study an actual intersection.

   a) Choose a traffic intersection in your community and measure the yellow light time and the width of the intersection.

   b) Draw a sketch of the intersection and include the GO Zone and the STOP Zone.

   c) Assume that human response time is 1.0 s and the deceleration rate is 5 m/s every second. Run the spreadsheet program with this data and find the STOP and GO Zones. You may also use a calculator and the appropriate equations.

   d) From your data, does a dilemma zone or an overlap zone exist? Is the intersection safe?

Observe the intersection from a safe distance. Follow all safety precautions set out by your teacher.

5. Assume that you have found a dangerous Dilemma Zone in a nearby intersection. As a good citizen, you would like to inform the Chamber of Commerce that the intersection is unsafe and that changing it will prevent some accidents and damage to property and people. You realize that the people at the Chamber of Commerce may not know about Go Zones and Stop Zones. You also know that you have a better chance of action if you are able to state the problem and suggest a solution.

   a) Prepare an outline of the information that should be included in the letter.

   b) Write the letter.

Activity Seven
Driving on Curves

WHAT DO YOU THINK?

You are driving along a road at the posted speed limit of 40 mph (20 m/s). A road sign warns that you are approaching a curve and tells you to slow down to 20 mph (10 m/s).

• **Why are they telling you to slow down?**

• **How do they know how much you should slow down?**

Record your ideas about these questions in your *Active Physics log*. Be prepared to discuss your responses with your small group and the class.

FOR YOU TO DO

1. Driving around a curve produces some special problems. Physics lets you model some of these problems. Imagine that you have a toy car at the end of a string, and it is moving in a circle. If you let go of the string, which way will the car go? The figure below gives you several choices.

✎ a) Choose in which direction you think the car will go.

   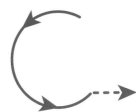

2. The best way to check your answer is to try it out. Tie a motorized toy car to a string about a half-meter long. With a finger, hold the other end of the string fixed to the tabletop. Turn on the car's motor, so that the car travels in a circle with your finger at the center, as shown in the diagram. Now release the string.

✎ a) Which way does the car travel when it is released?

✎ b) When a car makes a turn, what force keeps the car from going in a straight line? In what direction is the force?

✎ c) A car is traveling north. What is the direction of the force on the car when it is making a right turn?

TRANSPORTATION

3. To look at the factors that determine whether a car will stay on the road as it goes around a curve, you will do a second investigation. You will need a "lazy Susan" that you can turn, and a block of wood. Place a block of wood near the outer edge of the lazy Susan. Spin the lazy Susan. As it spins, the block is held in place by friction. This is not really the same as the traction that holds a car on the road, but it is similar.

4. Gradually increase the rotational speed of the lazy Susan until the block just begins to slide off. Now practice until you find the fastest speed where the block will stay in place. Determine the speed by measuring the time required for 10 revolutions.

   a) Record the number of revolutions per minute made by the lazy Susan when the friction is strong enough to keep the block going in a circle.

   b) How fast (revolutions per minute) is the lazy Susan turning when friction can no longer hold the block in place?

   c) How much time goes by during one revolution?

5. To find out how fast the block was going, you will need one other piece of information: the distance of the block from the center of the lazy Susan. Measure this in centimeters.

   a) Record your measurement.

6. To calculate the speed of an object you can divide the distance traveled by the time.

$$\text{Speed} = \frac{\text{distance}}{\text{time}}$$

When an object moves in a circle, the distance traveled in one revolution is the circumference of the circle.

Circumference = $2 \times \pi \times$ radius of circle

a) What was the speed of the block when it stayed on the lazy Susan? Slid off the lazy Susan?

Note: You may not be able to find the exact speed where the block leaves the lazy Susan. You can find a speed where the block stays in place and a speed where the block is not able to stay on the lazy Susan. You can call the first of these a "safe speed" and the second an "unsafe speed." Any speed lower than the "safe speed" will also be safe. Any speed higher than the "unsafe speed" will also be unsafe.

7. Place a rubber mat or some sandpaper between the block and the lazy Susan. Repeat the entire investigation.

a) Record all the necessary data.

b) Calculate the greatest speed at which the block can stay on the rubber mat.

c) How does the surface affect the maximum speed?

8. In addition to the speed and the road surface, you also need to look at the curvature of the road. Investigate this question by placing the block at various distances from the center of the lazy Susan.

a) What happens to the maximum speed as the radius of the path increases?

b) At each distance, find the maximum stable speed of the block.

REFLECTING ON THE ACTIVITY AND THE CHALLENGE

In this activity you learned that friction between the road and the tires helps keep the car on the road when it goes around a curve. More friction allows you to move faster and still stay on the road.

A tight turn requires more friction or a slower speed than a wider turn. Since you cannot change the friction on the road, a slower speed will keep the car on the road.

The challenge requires you to explain how driving around a curve may require a different speed than the normal speed limit. You may also want to explain what happens if the road conditions change, if your tires are in bad shape, or how the tightness of the turn also requires extra attention and a lower speed.

PHYSICS TO GO

1. A person at the equator travels once around the circumference of the earth in 24 hours. The radius of the earth is 6,400 km. How fast is the person going? Compute the speed in m/s and in km/h (one kilometer is equal to 1,000 m).

2. Earth travels in a circular motion around the sun. The radius of the Earth's motion is about 1.5×10^8 km. What is the speed of the Earth around the sun? Compute the speed in m/s and in km/h.

3. A fan turns at a rate of 60 revolutions per second. If the tip of the blade is 15 cm from the center, how fast is the tip moving?

4. Friction can hold a car on the road when it is traveling at 20 m/s and the radius of the turn is 15 m. What happens if

   a) the turn is tighter?
   b) the road surface gets slippery?
   c) both the turn is tighter and the road is more slippery?

5. Think about other examples in which objects travel in curved paths, such as the clothes in a spin-dryer, or the moon traveling around the earth. For each example, tell what produces the force that is constantly pushing the object toward the center of the curve.

6. Draw a graph showing the radial distance and the maximum speed at which the block remains on a lazy Susan for one type of surface.

7. The next time you feel "thrown out" of a car making a turn, explain to the driver that your body really wanted to go straight but that the car pulled you in. How did the driver react to your explanation?

8. Explain the following statement: "The driver may turn the wheels but it is the road that turns the car."

9. Write a few sentences telling your parents that you know how to apply the physics from this activity to drive safely around curves.

10. Use the information from this activity to write a statement about why you need to slow down around curves in rainy or icy weather.

INQUIRY INVESTIGATION

Design an experiment to determine if the mass of the car has an effect on the safe speed around a curve. After your teacher approves your procedure, conduct your investigation.

Activity Eight
Banking the Turns

WHAT DO YOU THINK?

On a race track, the curves are banked—the outer edge of the road is higher than the inner edge.

- **Why do you think the road is banked?**
- **Why is the outer edge of the road higher?**

Record your ideas about these questions in your *Active Physics log*. Be prepared to discuss your responses with your small group and the class.

FOR YOU TO DO

1. Place a wedge on your lazy Susan with its small end pointed toward the center of rotation. Use a piece of rubber mat under the wedge-shaped block of wood to increase the friction or hot glue the wedge to the Lazy Susan. Place your "car" or block of wood on the wedge.

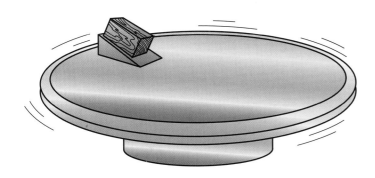

2. Spin the lazy Susan and find the maximum speed at which the friction on your test block is enough to keep the block from flying off the wedge.

   a) What is the highest speed at which the block remains on the banked roadbed?

   b) How does this compare with the speed when the block is held on by friction alone?

3. Reverse the position of the wedge to create a bank with the inner edge higher than the outer edge. Repeat the investigation.

   a) Record what happened.

   b) Why does the banking of the roadbed tend to keep the car on the curved road?

TRANSPORTATION

FOR YOU TO READ

Centripetal Force

As you saw with the toy car and the string, an object will travel in a straight line unless a force changes its direction. This is called The Law of Inertia, or NEWTON'S FIRST LAW: unless a force acts, an object will travel in a straight line at constant speed.

If something is traveling in a circular path, a force must act on it constantly, pulling it toward the center of the circle. Any force acting in this direction is called a centripetal force. You can see part of the word "center" in the word "centripetal." A centripetal force is always toward the center. For the toy car tied to a string, the centripetal force was supplied by the string. With the block on the turntable, the centripetal force is provided by the friction between the block and the turntable.

Why does banking the road provide more centripetal force? When a car is on a flat road, the road pushes up so that the car does not sink into the ground. When a car is on a banked road, the road surface keeps the car from sinking but also pushes toward the center of the curve. This push toward the center is a centripetal force.

If the car is going slow, this may be enough to keep it on the road. Let's say that the car needs a force of 20 N to keep it moving in a circle. The friction of a flat road surface must supply the entire 20 N. If the road is banked so that the road surface pushes the car toward the center, then the road surface may supply 15 N of the required 20 N of force. The friction of the road must supply only 5 N, giving the necessary total of 20 N.

A newton is a force unit, just like a meter is a length unit. One newton is approximately 1/4 lb. Yes, pounds also can be used to measure force. At McDonald's you could order a Newton Burger!

Centripetal Acceleration

Acceleration is the rate of change of velocity. This means that any change of speed or direction is an acceleration. There are three kinds of acceleration, each produced by a force:

A force applied in the direction of motion makes the object go faster.

A force applied against the direction of motion makes it go slower.

A force applied perpendicular to the direction of motion changes the direction without changing its speed. If a force acts continuously in a direction perpendicular to velocity, the object travels in a circle. The force, and the resulting acceleration, are then said to be centripetal.

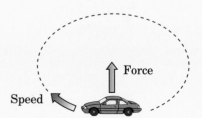

REFLECTING ON THE ACTIVITY
AND THE CHALLENGE

A banked turn helps to keep a car on the road when it goes around the curve. With a correctly banked curve, the road surface provides some of the centripetal force needed to make the turn. This means that if the road were to get slippery or icy, the banking of the road may provide the centripetal force to keep you from going off the road.

Explaining to your parents about banked roads is one part of the chapter challenge. You have performed experiments that can be used to illustrate your understanding of this road assist.

PHYSICS TO GO

1. Have you ever heard anyone brag about going around curves at speeds higher than the posted speed limit? How could they cheat the need for a large centripetal force? Is it by moving across lanes on the curve? Why is this not safe?

2. Why are indoor running tracks usually banked? Why are outdoor running tracks usually not banked?

3. a) How do runners turn fast corners on flat tracks?
   b) Where does a runner get centripetal force on a flat track?

4. Sometimes a road is banked the wrong way. Describe how a bank could be "the wrong way."

5. What happens if the road surface is banked so that road surface pushes you away from the center of the circle?

6. If there is a road in your neighborhood that is banked the wrong way, there are probably more traffic accidents there than at other locations. Explain why banking the road "the wrong way" makes driving more difficult.

STRETCHING EXERCISES

How much must a road be banked if gravity is to supply the same centripetal force as the friction? You cannot test this on a real road, but you can make a model of it with a wooden plank, a heavy object, a force meter, and a protractor.

1. Set the board in a horizontal position and put a brick or heavy block of wood on it.

2. Tie the brick to the force meter with string, and pull it along. When the brick is moving at a constant speed, the only force holding it back is the friction. The force meter is supplying the force needed to balance the friction. How much friction does the force meter indicate between the brick and the board?

⚠ If you set up this activity on a table, keep the equipment away from the edge of the table. If you are performing this activity on the floor, set it up in a low traffic area where no one is likely to trip over it.

3. Tilt the board by putting something under one end of it. In this position, the brick will have a tendency to slide downhill, due to the gravity. If you now pull it uphill at a constant speed, the force you exert is acting against both friction and the downhill pull of gravity. The force meter will now show the combined downhill forces of friction and gravity.

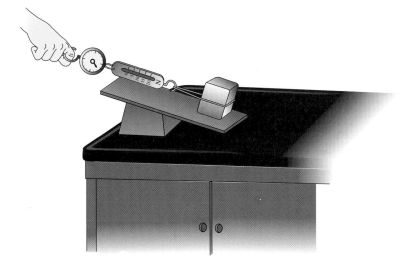

4. Your aim is to adjust the tilt so that the friction and the downhill pull of gravity are equal. You will know when this occurs because the force meter will read just twice as much as it did due to the effect of friction alone. At what angle of tilt are the forces of friction and gravity equal?

Will this experiment show a meaningful relationship between the forces of gravity and friction on a banked roadbed? Probably not. On a real road, much depends on the nature of the roadbed, the condition of the tires, the sharpness of the turn, and the speed of the car.

Activity Nine
Skids!

WHAT DO YOU THINK?

From 1989 to 1993, cars equipped with antilock braking systems were involved in fewer fatal front-end collisions. However, cars with these braking systems were involved in more nonfatal impacts with parked cars or fixed objects.

- **What is a skid? List a few examples.**
- **Why are you told not to brake when in a skid?**

Record your ideas about these questions in your *Active Physics log*. Be prepared to discuss your responses with your small group and the class.

FOR YOU TO DO

1. Use a small toy car without a motor and a ramp so that gravity supplies the force for putting the car into motion. Lock the rear wheels of the car with paper, a clamp, or a paper clip. Let the car roll down the ramp.

  a) Describe the motion of the car with the rear wheels locked.

2. Lock the front wheels and repeat the investigation.

  a) Describe the motion of the car with the front wheels locked.

3. Compare the motion of the car in the two situations.

  a) Use your knowledge of inertia and traction to explain what you observed.

4. You can use what you learned in this activity to predict what will happen to a car in other situations.

a) Predict what happens to the car if all four wheels lock.

b) Describe how you think the car would move if one tire "blew out."

c) Can you think of a way to test this with your toy car?

d) How would you expect a car to move if it loses traction from all four wheels on a curve? Remember that traction is similar to the friction you investigated in Activities 7 and 8.

e) What would be the motion of the car if only the rear wheels lose traction?

5. Watch the video of the race car driver demonstrating each skid. Complete the following for each type of skid you observe.

a) Draw a series of sketches that show the motion of the car during the skid.

b) Describe the motion of the car.

c) Write several sentences giving advice to a driver experiencing the skid.

6. Compare your observations with the toy car investigation and the skids observed on the video.

a) How were the motions the same? How were the motions different? Explain any differences.

FOR YOU TO READ

Skids can be grouped according to their cause:

Braking Skid: When brakes lock in either the front or the rear, the wheels stop turning, resulting in loss of friction. The skid can be in a forward direction or to either side.

Blowout Skid: When a tire blows out, this affects the traction the remaining tires have with the road.

This change in friction results in a sideways skid. The direction of the skid will depend on which tire blows.

Power Skid: Rapid acceleration (or deceleration) can result in "burning rubber." This reduces traction and results in the back of the car moving side to side, or "fishtailing."

Cornering Skid: This can happen during a turn at normal speeds if traction is reduced by pavement or tire conditions.

REFLECTING ON THE ACTIVITY AND THE CHALLENGE

Loss of traction, which is called skidding, happens when the tires stop rolling and begin to slide. There are different causes for skids, but all affect the motion of the car.

The chapter challenge does not require you to explain skids. You will not be asked to discuss why a front-wheel-drive car may be more stable than a rear-wheel-drive car. However, this information can increase your understanding of the physics of driving and help you become a better driver.

PHYSICS TO GO

1. Is a front-wheel-drive car more stable than a rear-wheel-drive car? Why or why not?

2. Consult the specification sheets for the Ford SVT Contour and the Chevrolet Corvette Convertible found on pages T55 and T56. Look for the weight distribution figures under the heading "General Data." Which of the two cars has its center of mass further forward? Why does this make a difference?

3. Look under "Chassis and Body" to find out which are the drive wheels. How would the drive wheel affect the behavior of the two cars under different conditions?

4. Select one of the main headings in the specification sheets for the two cars, and compare that feature in the two cars. Write a paragraph explaining why you would prefer one of the cars if that were the only consideration.

5. You can find safety facts and specifications for most cars and trucks by logging on to the National Highway Traffic Safety Administration's web page at http://www.nhtsa.dot.gov. What information can you use to find out which cars are the safest?

6. Use what you have learned about skids to convince your parents that you understand the physics of driving.

7. Combine your new understanding of skids with what you learned about going around curves to explain to a new driver how to react if he or she loses control of the car on a curve.

1998 Ford SVT CONTOUR

MANUFACTURER

Ford Motor Company
P.O Box 490
Dearborn, Mich. 48121

PRICE

List price.........................$22,900
Price as tested....................$23,635
    Price as tested includes std equip. (dual airbags, air cond, 16-in. alloy wheels and 205/55ZR-16 tires, leather interior, AM/FM stereo/cassette; pwr windows, seats, door locks & mirrors; dest charge), pwr sunroof ($595), CD player ($140).

0—60 mph	7.2 sec
0—¼ mi	15.4 sec
Top speed	est 143 mph
Skidpad	0.83g
Slalom	61.9 mph
Brake rating	excellent

TEST CONDITIONS

Temperature.........................70° F
Wind..................................calm
Elevation..........................1010 ft

SCALE: 10 in. (254mm) DIVISIONS
DRAWING BY BILL DOBSON

ENGINE

Type... aluminum block and heads, **V-6**
Valvetrain..........dohc 4 valve/cyl
Displacement.....155 cu in./2544 cc
Bore x stroke.......3.24 x 3.11 in./
                     82.4 x 79.0 mm
Compression ratio...........10.0:1
Horsepower
    (SAE).......**195 bhp @ 6625 rpm**
Bhp/liter.....................76.7
Torque.......**165 lb-ft @ 5625 rpm**
Maximum engine speed.....6750 rpm
Fuel injection....elect. sequential port
Fuel.....prem unleaded, 91 pump oct

CHASSIS & BODY

Layout......**front engine/front drive**
Body/frame.............unit steel
Brakes
    Front........**10.9-in. vented discs**
    Rear.........**9.9-in. vented discs**
    Assist type..........vacuum; ABS
    Total swept area.......366 sq in.
    Swept area/ton.......230 sq in.
Wheels.........cast alloy, **16 x 6½**
Tires.........Goodyear Eagle GS-C,
                        P205/55ZR-16
Steering...**rack & pinion**, power assist
    Overall ratio...............14.5:1
    Turns, lock to lock...........2.7
    Turning circle.............38.4 ft
Suspension
    Front........**MacPherson struts,**
        lower A-arms, coil springs,
        tube shocks, anti-roll bar
    Rear.....**struts,** trailing links, dual
        lower lateral links, coil springs,
        tube shocks, anti-roll bar

DRIVETRAIN

Transmission.........................**5-sp manual**

Gear	Ratio	Overall ratio	(Rpm) Mph
1st	3.42:1	13.89:1	(6750) 34
2nd	2.14:1	8.69:1	(6750) 55
3rd	1.45:1	5.89:1	(6750) 81
4th	1.03:1	4.18:1	(6750) 114
5th	0.77:1	3.13:1	est (6310) 143

Final drive ratio...................4.06:1
Engine rpm @ 60 mph in 5th............2650

GENERAL DATA

Curb weight..............**3055 lb**
Test weight..............3180 lb
Weight dist (with
    driver), f/r, %..........63/37
Wheelbase.............106.5 in.
Track, f/r.....59.2 in./58.5 in.
Length.................**183.9 in.**
Width..................69.1 in.
Height.................54.5 in.
Ground clearance...........8.2 in.
Trunk space........18.0 + 7.0 cu ft

MAINTENANCE

Oil/filter change....5000 mi/5000mi
Tuneup................100,000 mi
Basic warranty.....36 mo/36,000 mi

ACCOMMODATIONS

Seating capacity................5
Head room, f/r.....39.0 in./35.0 in.
Seat width, f/r...2 x 20.5 in./50.0 in.
Front-seat leg room..........43.0 in.
Rear-seat knee room..........25.0 in.
Seatback adjustment........85 deg
Seat travel.................8.5 in.

INTERIOR NOISE

Idle in neutral.............54 dBA
Maximum in 1st gear.......78 dBA
Constant 50 mph..........66 dBA
70 mph...................71 dBA

INSTRUMENTATION

160-mph speedometer, 8000-rpm tach,
coolant temp, fuel level

ACCELERATION

Time to speed	Seconds
0–30 mph	2.5
0–40 mph	3.8
0–50 mph	5.2
0–60 mph	7.2
0–70 mph	9.3
0–80 mph	11.6
0–90 mph	14.8
0–100 mph	18.8

Time to distance	
0–100 ft	3.3
0–500 ft	8.4
0–1320 ft (¼ mi):	15.4 @ 91.5 mph

FUEL ECONOMY

Normal driving...........20.0 mpg
EPA city/highway.......20/29 mpg
Cruise range.............270 miles
Fuel capacity..........14.5 gal.

BRAKING

Minimum stopping distance
    From 60 mph............135 ft
    From 80 mph............228 ft
Control..................excellent
Pedal effort for 0.5g stop.......na
Fade, effort after six 0.5g stops from
    60 mph...................na
Brake feel..............excellent
Overall brake rating........excellent

HANDLING

Lateral accel (200-ft skidpad)...0.83g
    Balance.......moderate understeer
Speed thru 700-ft slalom....61.9 mph
    Balance..........mild understeer
Lateral seat support.......very good

Subjective ratings consist of excellent, very good, good, average, poor; na means information is not available.

Test Notes...

■ Around the skidpad, the SVT Contour moderately understeers, though its cornering attitude is quite responsive to lifting the throttle. Indeed, it reacts even more strongly to light brake taps.

■ Through the slalom, the SVT Contour is again highly responsive to throttle and impressively placeable. Body roll is considerable, but it doesn't slow the Contour's reflexes.

■ Although it offers no more torque than the V-6-powered Contour SE, and most of its extra power is near redline, the SVT's 195-bhp engine sounds wonderful and is extremely flexible.

JULY 1997 **93**

1998 Chevrolet CORVETTE CONVERTIBLE

MANUFACTURER

Chevrolet Motor Division
30007 Van Dyke Road
Warren, Mich. 48090

PRICE

List price	est $44,990
Price as tested	est $54,554

Price as tested includes std equip. (dual airbags, cruise control, ABS, traction control, security system, removable roof panel, AM/FM stereo/cassette, pwr windows & mirrors), magnesium wheels (est $3000), F45 Real-Time Damping Suspension (est $1700), Preferred Equip. Pkg 1 (includes central locking and dual temp control) est $1330, leather pwr adj sport seats (est $1200), CD player/changer (est $395), luxury tax (est $1374), dest charge (est $565).

0–60 mph	**5.2 sec**
0–¼ mi	**13.8 sec**
Top speed	**est 165 mph**
Skidpad	**na**
Slalom	**62.5 mph**
Brake rating	**excellent**

TEST CONDITIONS

Temperature	86° F
Wind	calm
Elevation	est 700 ft

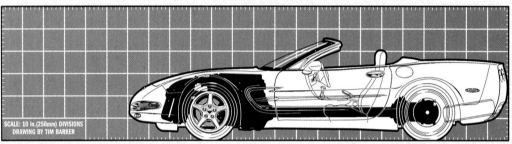

SCALE: 10 in.(250mm) DIVISIONS
DRAWING BY TIM BARKER

ENGINE

Type	aluminum block and heads, **V-8**
Valvetrain	ohv 2 valve/cyl
Displacement	346 cu in./5666 cc
Bore x stroke	3.90 x 3.62 in./ 99.0 x 92.0 mm
Compression ratio	10.1:1
Horsepower (SAE)	**345 bhp @ 5600 rpm**
Bhp/liter	60.9
Torque	**350 lb-ft @ 4400 rpm**
Maximum engine speed	6000 rpm
Fuel injection	elect. sequential port
Fuel	prem unleaded, 91 pump oct

CHASSIS & BODY

Layout	**front engine/rear drive**
Body/frame	fiberglass/ steel unit frame

Brakes
Front	**12.8-in. vented discs**
Rear	**12.0-in. vented discs**
Assist type	vacuum; ABS
Total swept area	433 sq in.
Swept area/ton	257 sq in.
Wheels	cast magnesium; **17 x 8½ f, 18 x 9½ r**
Tires	Goodyear Eagle F1; **P245/45ZR-17 f, P275/40ZR-18 r**
Steering	**rack & pinion,** variable power assist
Overall ratio	16.1:1
Turns, lock to lock	2.7
Turning circle	38.5 ft

Suspension
Front	**upper & lower A-arms,** transverse composite monoleaf spring, tube shocks, anti-roll bar
Rear	**upper & lower A-arms,** toe links, transverse composite monoleaf spring, tube shocks, anti-roll bar

DRIVETRAIN

Transmission ... **6-sp manual**

Gear	Ratio	Overall ratio	(Rpm) Mph
1st	2.66:1	9.10:1	(6000) 52
2nd	1.78:1	6.09:1	(6000) 77
3rd	1.30:1	4.45:1	(6000) 105
4th	1.00:1	3.42:1	(6000) 137
5th	0.74:1	2.53:1	est (5365) 165
6th	0.50:1	1.71:1	est (3625) 165

Final drive ratio	3.42:1
Engine rpm @ 60 mph in 6th	1320

GENERAL DATA

Curb weight	**est 3240 lb**
Test weight	est 3380 lb
Weight dist (with driver), f/r, %	51/49
Wheelbase	104.5 in.
Track, f/r	62.0 in./62.0 in.
Length	**179.7 in.**
Width	**73.6 in.**
Height	**47.7 in.**
Ground clearance	3.7 in.
Trunk space	13.5 cu ft (top up)/ 10.8 cu ft (top down)

MAINTENANCE

Oil/filter change	7500 mi/7500 mi
Tuneup	100,000 mi
Basic warranty	36 mo/36,000 mi

ACCOMMODATIONS

Seating capacity	**2**
Head room	36.5 in.
Seat width	2 x 18.0 in.
Leg room	43.5 in.
Seatback adjustment	45 deg
Seat travel	8.0 in.

INTERIOR NOISE

Idle in neutral	61 dBA
Maximum in 1st gear	78 dBA
Constant 50 mph	73 dBA
70 mph	76 dBA

INSTRUMENTATION

200-mph speedometer, 7500-rpm tach, coolant temp, fuel level, volts, oil press.

ACCELERATION

Time to speed	Seconds
0–30 mph	2.0
0–40 mph	2.9
0–50 mph	4.2
0–60 mph	5.2
0–70 mph	6.6
0–80 mph	8.7
0–90 mph	10.9
0–100 mph	13.3

Time to distance
0–100 ft	3.0
0–500 ft	7.5
0–1320 ft (¼ mi)	13.8 @ 102.1 mph

FUEL ECONOMY

Normal driving	est 18.5 mpg
EPA city/highway	18/28 mpg
Cruise range	est 335 miles
Fuel capacity	19.1 gal.

BRAKING

Minimum stopping distance
From 60 mph	118 ft
From 80 mph	209 ft
Control	excellent
Pedal effort for 0.5g stop	na
Fade, effort after six 0.5g stops from 60 mph	na
Brake feel	excellent
Overall brake rating	excellent

HANDLING

Lateral accel (200-ft skidpad)	na
Balance	na
Speed thru 700-ft slalom	62.5 mph
Balance	moderate understeer
Lateral seat support	excellent

Test Notes...

■ Through the slalom, the convertible's P275/40ZR-18 rear tires helped make quick work of the cones. Even near the limit of rear adhesion, a quick burst of the throttle settles the tail back in line.

■ Quick acceleration times in the Vette require the right combination of engine rpm and clutch modulation. Dropping the clutch at 3000 rpm gave just enough wheelspin to produce the best run of the day.

■ At cruising speeds, the convertible is predictably noisier than the coupe. Especially noticeable is the thumping of the big rear tires on the road, heard through the open cargo area behind the seats.

SEPTEMBER 1997 **71**

PHYSICS AT WORK

Sara Senske

RACE CAR DRIVING IS HER PASSION

"When I'm banking a curve at 130 mph," states Sara, an 18-year-old race car champion, "time slows down and takes on a new perspective. I feel in complete control."

Sara has been racing cars since she was 7 and has participated in nine Grand National races. "I won my first race when I was seven, and I've been focused on racing as a career ever since. I knew it was going to be tough, but my dream is to be the first woman to climb the ranks of pro racing and to open the door for other women to get into the sport." Her father, a retired racing champion, was her first coach and continues to be very involved in her career. It was her father that first taught her about acceleration, stopping reaction time and banking curves.

Sara has recently been signed onto the prestigious Lynx Racing Team as their first female driver and will race for them this year in the Star Formula Mazda Championships. The Lynx Racing Team seeks out young racing drivers with championship potential and provides them with the resources and training they need to jump to the top levels of motor sports. "Lynx has a reputation among racers for signing top drivers and teaching them to be champions, and in my heart, I've always felt like a champion, " says Sara.

Sara keeps up an extensive daily physical training regime to help maintain the quick reflexes needed for car racing. "I've always loved the feeling of control I get when I'm driving a race car and the adrenaline rush of the speed," states Sara. In order to gain that control, win races, and survive a dangerous sport, Sara has had to developed a keen knowledge and understanding of the physical principals of the road. "Education, beginning with the basics, and going on to the minor detail understood by only a few, is the foundation of the Lynx Racing program," states Steve Cameron the team's manager. "Our goal, and hers, is for her to make it to Indy cars, not because she is a woman, but because she is a great driver."

Chapter Assessment

You will be assigned to a group of 3. You will have a sheet of paper that lists the content of this chapter. Three columns will be drawn next to each area of content. The first column is to be used if the student is able to explain to the other two students, the "parents," the content with no help. The middle column is to be used if the student needs some help from the "parents". The third column is to be used if the student needs lots of help from the "parents." The letter to be placed in each column is an E (excellent), G (good), or S (satisfactory). Place your name on the top of the sheet. Hand the sheet to the two "parents" who will assess the quality of the explanations.

1. Explain to your "parents":
   a) The effect of response time.
   b) Safe following distances.
   c) How stopping distance depends on speed.
   d) How to decide what to do at a yellow light.
   e) How you have to change your speed around a curve.

2. Write a letter to a traffic engineer about an unsafe intersection. Describe your observations and calculations to support your concern about safety. Include questions you would like to have answered and suggestions for ways to decrease the potential danger at that intersection.

3. Make a presentation to a beginning driver about how distractions or alcohol affect response time.

4. Calculate:
   a) Stopping distance for given speeds.
   b) Whether the light cycle at an intersection is safe.

5. Create an advertisement, cartoon, or story that tells about one issue of safe driving.

Review the criteria for success that were discussed at the beginning of this chapter.

Physics You Learned

Estimate and measurement of response time

Series circuit

Graphing

Distance, velocity, time

Distance vs. time graphs with the sonic ranger

Stopping distance

Yellow light dilemma

Spreadsheet modeling

Circular motion

Centripetal force

Banked curves

Skidding

SAFETY

Scenario

Probably the most dangerous thing you will do today is travel to your destination. Transportation is necessary, but the need to get there in a hurry, and the large number of people and vehicles, have made transportation very risky. There is a greater chance of being killed or injured traveling than in any other common activity. Realizing this, people and governments have begun to take action to alter the statistics. New safety systems have been designed and put into use in automobiles and airplanes. New laws and a new awareness are working together with these systems to reduce the danger in traveling.

What are these new safety systems? You are probably familiar with many of them. In this chapter, you will become more familiar with most of these designs. Could you design or even build a better safety device for a car or a plane? Many students around the country have been doing just that, and with great success!

Challenge

Your design team will develop a safety system for protecting automobile, airplane, bicycle, motorcycle, or train passengers. As you study existing safety systems, you and your design team should be listing ideas for improving an existing system or designing a new system for preventing accidents. You may also consider a system that will minimize the harm caused by accidents.

Your final product will be a working model or prototype of a safety system. On the day that you bring the final product to class, the teams will display them around the room while class members informally view them and discuss them with members of the design team. During this time, class members will ask questions about each others products. The questions will be placed in envelopes provided to each team by the teacher. The teacher will use some of these questions during the oral presentations on the next day.

The product will be judged according to the following three parts:

1. The quality of your safety feature enhancement and the working model or prototype.

2. The quality of a 5-minute oral report that should include:

   • **the need for the system;**
   • **the method used to develop the working model;**
   • **the demonstration of the working model;**
   • **the discussion of the physics concepts involved;**
   • **the description of the next-generation version of the system;**
   • **the answers to questions posed by the class.**

3. The quality of a written and/or multimedia report including:

   • **the information from the oral report;**
   • **the documentation of the sources of expert information;**
   • **the discussion of consumer acceptance and market potential;**
   • **the discussion of the physics concepts applied in the design of the safety system.**

Criteria

You and your classmates will work with your teacher to define the criteria for determining grades. You will also be asked to evaluate your own work. Discuss as a class the performance task and the points that should be allocated for each part. A starting point for your discussions may be:

• **Part 1 = 40 points**
• **Part 2 = 30 points**
• **Part 3 = 30 points**

Since group work is made up of individual work, your teacher will assign some points to each individual's contribution to the project. If individual points total 30 points, then parts 1, 2 and 3 must be changed so that the total remains at 100.

Activity One

Accidents

WHAT DO YOU THINK?

Chances are you will not be able to avoid being in an accident at some time in the future.

- **How can you protect yourself from serious injury, or even death, should an accident occur?**

- **What do you think is the greatest danger to you or the people in an accident?**

Record your ideas about these questions in your *Active Physics log*. Be prepared to discuss your responses with your small group and the class.

FOR YOU TO DO

1. Many people think that they know the risks involved with day-to-day transportation. The "test" below will check your knowledge of automobile accidents. The statements are organized in a true and false format. Record a T in your log for each statement you believe is true and an F if you believe the statement is false. Your teacher will supply the correct answers for discussion at the end of the activity.

   a) More people die because of cancer than automobile accidents.
   b) Your chances of surviving a collision improve if you are thrown from the car.
   c) The fatality rate of motorcycle accidents is less than that of cars.
   d) A large number of people who are belted into their cars are killed in a burning or submerged car.
   e) If you don't have a child restraint seat, you should place the child in your seat belt with you.
   f) You can react fast enough during an accident to brace yourself in the car seat.
   g) Most people die in traffic accidents during long trips.
   h) A person not wearing a seat belt in your car poses a hazard to you.
   i) Traffic accidents occur most often on Monday mornings.
   j) Male drivers between the ages of 16 and 19 are most likely to be involved in traffic accidents.
   k) Casualty collisions are most frequent during the winter months due to snow and ice.
   l) More pedestrians than drivers are killed by cars.
   m) The greatest number of roadway fatalities can be attributed to poor driving conditions.
   n) The greatest number of females involved in traffic accidents are between the ages of 16 and 20.
   o) Unrestrained occupant casualties are more likely to be young adults between the ages of 16 and 19.

2. Calculate your score. Give yourself two points for a correct answer, and subtract one point for an incorrect answer. You might want to match your score against the descriptors given below.

21 to 30 points: Expert Analyst

14 to 20 points: Assistant Analyst

9 to 13 points: Novice Analyst

8 points and below: Myth Believer

a) Record your score in your log. Were you surprised about the extent of your knowledge? Some of the reasons behind these facts will be better understood as you travel through this chapter.

⚠️ **Obtain permission from the cars' owners before proceeding.**

3. Survey at least three different cars for safety features. The list on the next page will allow you to evaluate the safety features of each of the cars. Place a check mark in the appropriate square.

Number 1 indicates very poor or nonexistent, 2 is minimum standard, 3 is average, 4 is good, and 5 is very good.

For example, when rating air bags: a car with no air bags could be given a 1 rating, a car with only a driver-side air bag a 2, a car with driver and passenger side air bags a 3, a car with slow release driver and passenger-side air bags a 4, and a car which includes side-door air bags to the previous list a 5. You may add additional safety features not identified in the chart. Many additional features can be added!

a) Copy and complete the table in your log.

b) Which car would you evaluate as being safest?

Car Tested: Make and Model _____	Year _____				
Safety Feature	Rating				
Padded front seats	1	2	3	4	5
Padded roof frame	1	2	3	4	5
Head rests	1	2	3	4	5
Knee protection	1	2	3	4	5
Anti-daze rear-view mirror that brakes on impact	1	2	3	4	5
Child proof safety locks on rear doors	1	2	3	4	5
Padded console	1	2	3	4	5
Padded sun visor	1	2	3	4	5
Padded doors and arm rests	1	2	3	4	5
Steering wheel with padded rim and hub	1	2	3	4	5
Padded gear level					
Padded door pillars					
Air bags					

REFLECTING ON THE ACTIVITY AND CHALLENGE

Serious injuries in an automobile accident have many causes. If there are no restraints or safety devices in a vehicle, or if the vehicle is not constructed to absorb any of the energy of the collision, even a minor collision can cause serious injury. Until the early 1960's, automobile design and construction did not even consider passenger safety. The general belief was that a heavy car was a safe car. While there is some truth to that statement, today's lighter cars are far safer than the "tanks" of the past.

The safety survey may have provided ideas for constructing a prototype of a safety system used for transportation. If it has, write down ideas in your log that have been generated from this activity.

PHYSICS TO GO

1. Review and list all the safety features found in today's new cars. As you compile your list, write next to each safety feature one or more of the following designations:

   F: effective in a front-end collision.

   R: effective in a rear-end collision.

   S: effective in a collision where the car is struck on the side.

   T: effective when the car rolls over or turns over onto its roof.

2. Make a list of safety features that could be used for cycling.

3. Make a list of safety features that could be used for in-line skating.

4. Make a list of safety features that could be used for skate boarding.

5. Ask family members or friends if you may evaluate their car. Discuss and explain your evaluation to the car owners. Record your evaluation and their response in your log.

STRETCHING EXERCISES

1. Read a consumer report on car safety. Are any cars on the road particularly unsafe?

2. Collect brochures from various automobile dealers. What new safety features are presented in the brochures? How much of the advertising is devoted to safety?

Activity Two
Life [and Death] before Seat Belts

WHAT DO YOU THINK?

Throughout most of the country, the law requires automobile passengers to wear seat belts.

- **Should wearing a seat belt be a personal choice?**
- **What are two reasons why there should be seat belt laws and two reasons why there should not?**

Record your ideas about these questions in your *Active Physics log*. Be prepared to discuss your responses with your small group and the class.

FOR YOU TO DO

1. In this activity, you will investigate car crashes where the driver or passenger does not wear seat belts. Your model car is a laboratory cart. Your model passenger is molded from a lump of soft clay. With the "passenger" in place, send the "car" at a low speed into a wall.

✎a) Describe, in your log, what happens to the "passenger."

⚠ **Perform the activity outside of traffic areas. Do not obstruct paths to exits. Do not leave carts lying on the floor.**

TRANSPORTATION

2. Repeat the collision at a high speed. Compare and contrast this collision with the previous one.

  a) Compare and contrast requires you to find and record at least one similarity and one difference. A better response includes more similarities and differences.

3. You can conduct a more analytical experiment by having the cart hit the wall at varying speeds. Set up a ramp on which the car can travel. Release the car on the ramp and observe as it crashes into the wall. Repeat the collision for at least two ramp heights.

  a) Record the heights of the ramp and describe the results of the collision. Describe the collision by noting the damage to the "passenger."

PHYSICS TALK

Newton's First Law of Motion

Newton's First Law of Motion (also called the Law of Inertia) is one of the foundations of physics. It states:

An object at rest stays at rest, and an object in motion stays in motion unless acted upon by a force.

There are three distinct parts to Newton's First Law.

Part 1 says that objects at rest stay at rest. This hardly seems surprising.

Part 2 says that objects in motion stay in motion. This may seem strange indeed. After looking at the collisions of this activity, this should seem clearer.

Part 3 says that parts 1 and 2 are only true when no force is present.

FOR YOU TO READ

Three Collisions in One Accident!

Arthur C. Damask analyzes automobile accidents and deaths for insurance companies and police reports. This is how Professor Damask describes an accident:

Consider the occupants of a conveyance moving at some speed. If the conveyance strikes an object, it will rapidly decelerate to some lower speed or stop entirely; this is called the first collision. But the occupants have been moving at the same speed, and will continue to do so until they are stopped by striking the interior parts of the car (if not ejected); this is the second collision. The brain and body organs have also been moving at the same speed and will continue to do so until they are stopped by colliding with the shell of the body, i.e., the interior of the skull, the thoracic cavity, and the abdominal wall. This is called the third collision.

Newton's First Law of Motion explains the three collisions:

- First collision: the car strikes the pole; the pole exerts the force that brings the car to rest.
- Second collision: when the car stops, the body keeps moving; the structure of the car exerts the force that brings the body to rest.
- Third collision: the body stops, but the heart and brain keep moving; the body wall exerts the force that brings the heart and brain to rest.

Even with all the safety features in our automobiles, some deaths cannot be prevented. In one accident, only a single car was involved, with only the driver inside. The car failed to follow the road around a turn, and it struck a telephone pole. The seat belt and the air bag prevented any serious injuries apart from a few bruises, but the driver died. An autopsy showed that the driver's aorta had burst, at the point where it leaves the heart.

REFLECTING ON THE ACTIVITY AND THE CHALLENGE

In this activity you discovered that an object in motion continues in motion until a force stops it. A car will stop when it hits a pole but the passenger will keep on moving. If the car and passenger have a large speed, then the passenger will continue moving with this large speed. The passenger at the large speed will experience more damage from the fast moving cart.

Have you ever heard someone say that they can prevent an injury by bracing themselves against the crash? They can't! Restraining devices help provide support. Without a restraining system, the force of impact is either absorbed by the rib, skull, or brain.

Use Newton's First Law of motion to describe your design. How will your safety system protect passengers from low speed and higher speed collisions?

PHYSICS TO GO

1. Describe how Newton's First Law applies to the following situations:

   • You step on the brakes to stop your car.

   (Sample answer: You and the car are moving forward. The brakes apply a force to the tires and stop them from rotating. Newton's law states that an object in motion will remain in motion unless a force acts upon it. In this case, the force is friction between the ground and the tires. You remain in motion since the force that stopped the car did not stop you.)

   • You step on the accelerator to get going.

   • You turn the wheel to go around a curve. (Hint: You keep moving in a straight line.)

   • You step on the brakes, and an object in the back of the car comes flying forward.

2. Give two more examples of how Newton's First Law applies to vehicles or people in motion.

3. According to Newton's First Law, objects in motion will continue in motion unless acted upon by a force. Using Newton's First Law, explain why a cart that rolls down a ramp eventually comes to rest.

4. The skateboard, shown in the picture to the right, strikes the curb. Draw a diagram indicating the direction in which the person moves. Use Newton's First Law to explain the direction of movement.

5. Explain, in your own words, the three collisions during a single crash as described by Professor Damask in For You to Read.

6. Use the diagrams below to compare the second and third collisions described by Professor Damask with the impact of a punch during a boxing match.

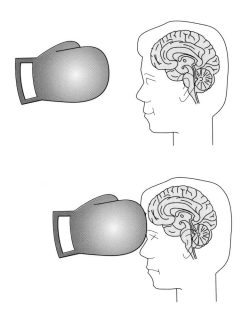

7. When was the law instituted requiring drivers to wear seat belts?

TRANSPORTATION

STRETCHING EXERCISE

1. Determine what opinions people in your community hold about the wearing of seat belts. Compare the opinions of the +60 years old and 25 to 59 years old groups with that of the 15 to 24 year old group. Survey at least five people in each age group: Group A = 15 to 24 years, Group B = 25 to 59 years, and Group C = 60 years and older. (Survey the same number of individuals in each age group.) Ask each individual to fill out a survey card.

A sample questionnaire is provided below. You may wish to eliminate any question that you feel is not relevant. You are encouraged to develop questions of your own that help you understand what attitudes people in your community hold about wearing seat belts. The answers have been divided into three categories: 1 = agree; 2 = will accept , but do not hold a strong opinion; and 3 = disagree. Try to keep your survey to between five and ten questions.

Age group:	Date of Survey:		
Statement	Agree	No strong opinion	Disagree
1. I believe people should be fined for not wearing seat belts.	1	2	3
2. I wouldn't wear a seat belt if I didn't have to.	1	2	3
3. People who don't wear seat belts pose a threat to me when they ride in my car.	1	2	3
4. I believe that seat belts save lives.	1	2	3
5. Seat belts wrinkle my clothes and fit poorly so I don't wear them.	1	2	3

2. Make a list of reasons why people refuse to wear seat belts. Can you challenge these opinions using what you have learned about Newton's First Law of Motion?

Activity Three

Life (and Fewer Deaths) after Seat Belts

WHAT DO YOU THINK?

In a collision, you cannot brace yourself and prevent injuries. Your arms and legs are not strong enough to overcome the inertia during even a minor collision. Instead of thinking about stopping yourself when the car is going 30 mph, think about catching 10 bowling balls hurtling towards you at 30 mph. The two situations are equivalent.

• **Suppose you had to design seat belts for a race car that can go 200 mph. How would they be different from the ones available on passenger cars?**

Record your ideas about this question in your *Active Physics log*. Be prepared to discuss your responses with your small group and the class.

TRANSPORTATION

FOR YOU TO DO

1. In this activity you will test different materials for their suitability for use as seat belts. Your model car is, once again, a laboratory cart; your model passenger is molded from a lump of soft clay. Give your passenger a seat belt by stretching a thin piece of wire across the front of the passenger, and attaching it on the sides or rear of the car.

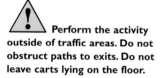 **Perform the activity outside of traffic areas. Do not obstruct paths to exits. Do not leave carts lying on the floor.**

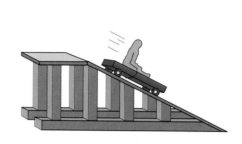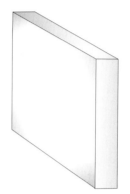

2. Make a collision by sending the car down a ramp. Start with small angles of incline and increase the height of the ramp until you see significant injury to the clay passenger.

   a) In your log, note the height of the ramp at which significant injury occurs.

3. Use at least two other kinds of seat belts (ribbons, cloth, etc.). Begin by using the same incline of ramp and release height as in step 2.

   a) In your log, record the ramp height at which significant injury occurs to the "passenger" using the other kinds of seat belt material.

4. Crash dummies cost $50,000! Watch the video presentation of a car in a collision, with a dummy in the driver's seat. You may have to observe it more than once to answer the following questions.

   a) In the collision, the car stops abruptly. What happens to the driver?

   b) What parts of the driver's body are in the greatest danger? Explain what you saw in terms of the law of inertia (Newton's First Law of Motion).

FOR YOU TO READ

Force and Pressure

When you repeated this experiment accurately each time, the force that each belt exerted on the clay was the same each time that the car was started at the same ramp height. Yet different materials have different effects; for example, a wire cuts far more deeply into the clay than a broader material does.

The force that each of the belts exerts on the clay is the same. When a thin wire is used, all the force is concentrated onto a small area. By replacing the wire with a broader material, you spread the force out over a much larger area of contact.

The force per unit area, which is called pressure, is much smaller with a ribbon, for example, than with a wire. It is the pressure, not the force, that determines how much damage the seat belt does to the body. A force applied to a single rib might be enough to break a rib. If the same force is spread out over many ribs, the force on each rib can be made too small to do any damage. While the total force does not change, the pressure becomes much smaller.

PHYSICS TALK

Pressure is the force per unit area:

$$P = F/A$$

where F represents force, measured in newtons (N); A represents area, determined in meters squared (m^2); and P is pressure calculated in newtons per meter squared (N/m^2).

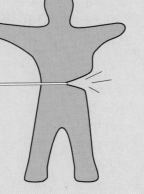

Force can be measured using a spring scale.

TRANSPORTATION

Example

Why does the boy without snow shoes sink into the snow? The relationship between force and area can be expressed as pressure. Because both boys have the same mass, a constant force of 450 N is applied to the snow. The first boy, wearing snow shoes, stands on a much wider base (2.0 m^2), while the second boy has a much smaller base (0.1 m^2).

Boy A Pressure = $\frac{\text{Force}}{\text{Area}}$ Boy B Pressure = $\frac{\text{Force}}{\text{Area}}$

$P = \frac{450 \text{ N}}{2.0 \text{ m}^2}$ $P = \frac{450 \text{ N}}{0.1 \text{ m}^2}$

$P = 225 \text{ N/m}^2$ $P = 4500 \text{ N/m}^2$

REFLECTING ON THE ACTIVITY

In this activity you gathered data to provide evidence on the effectiveness of seat belts as restraint systems. The material used for the seat belt and the width of the restraint affected the distortion of the clay figure. By applying the force over a greater area, the pressure exerted by the seat belt during the collision can be reduced.

It is important to note that not every safety restraint system will be a seat belt or harness, but that all restraints attempt to reduce the pressure exerted on an object by increasing the area over which a force is applied.

How will your design team account for decreasing pressure by increasing the area of impact? Think about ways that you could test your design prototype for the pressure created during impact. Your presentation of the design will be much more convincing if you have quantitative data to support your claims. Simply stating that a safety system works well is not as convincing as being able to show how it reduces pressure during a collision.

PHYSICS TO GO

1. Use Newton's First Law to describe a collision with the passenger wearing a seat belt during a collision.

2. What is the pressure exerted when a force of 10 N is applied to an object that has an area of

   a) $1.0 \ m^2$?

   b) $0.2 \ m^2$?

   c) $15 \ m^2$?

   d) $400 \ cm^2$?

3. A person who weights approximately 155 lb. exerts 700 N of force on the ground while standing. If his shoes cover an area of $400 \ cm^2$ ($0.0400 \ m^2$), calculate:

   a) the average pressure his shoes exert on the ground.

   b) the pressure he would exert by standing on one foot.

4. For comparison purposes, calculate the pressure you exert in the situations described below. Divide your weight in newtons, by the area of your shoes. (To find your weight in newtons multiply your weight in pounds by 4.5 N/lb. You can approximate the area of your shoes by tracing the soles on a sheet of centimeter squared paper.)

   a) How much pressure would you exert if you were standing in high heels?

   b) How much pressure would you exert while standing on your hands?

   c) If a bed of nails contains 5000 nails per square meter, how much force would one nail support if you were to lie on the bed? With this calculation you can now explain how people are able to lie on a bed of nails. It's just physics!

5. Describe why a wire seat belt would not be effective even though the force exerted on you by the wire seat belt is identical to that of a cloth seat belt.

6. Do you think there ought to be seat belt laws? How does not using seat belts affect the society as a whole?

7. Conduct a survey of 10 people. Ask each person what percentage of the time they wear a seat belt while in a car. Be prepared to share your data with the class.

STRETCHING EXERCISES

The pressure exerted on your clay model by a thin wire can be estimated quite easily. Loop the wire around the "passenger," and connect the wire to a force meter.

   a) Pull the force meter hard enough to make the wire sink into the model just about as far as it did in the collision.

   b) Record the force as shown on the force meter (in newtons).

   c) Estimate the frontal area of the wire—its diameter times the length of the wire that contacts the passenger. Record this value in centimeters squared (cm^2).

   d) Divide the force by the area. This is the pressure in newtons per centimeter squared (N/cm^2).

Activity Four
Why Air Bags?

WHAT DO YOU THINK?

Air bags do not take the place of seat belts. Air bags are an additional protection. They are intended to be used with seat belts to increase safety.

- **Why are air bags effective?**
- **How does the air bag protect you?**

Record your ideas about these questions in your *Active Physics log*. Be prepared to discuss your responses with your small group and the class.

FOR YOU TO DO

1. You will use a large plastic bag or a partially inflated beach ball as a model for an air bag. Impact is provided by a heavy steel ball, or just a good-sized rock, dropped from a height of a couple of meters. Gather the equipment you will need for this activity. Your problem is to find out how long it takes the object to come to rest. What is the total time duration from when the object first touches the air bag until it bounces back?

TRANSPORTATION

2. With a camcorder, videotape the object striking the air bag from a given height such as 1.5 m.

✎ a) Record the exact height from which you dropped the object.

3. Play the sequence back, one frame at a time. Count the number of frames during the time the object is moving into the air bag—from the moment it first touches the bag until it comes to rest, before bouncing. Each frame stands for $\frac{1}{30}$ s. (Check your manual.)

✎ a) In your log, record the number of frames and calculate how long it takes for the object to come to rest.

If a camcorder is not available, the experiment may be performed, although less effectively, by attaching a ticker-tape timer to the falling object.

After the object is dropped, with the object still attached, stretch the tape from the release position to the air bag. Mark the dot on the tape that was made just as the object touched the air bag.

Now push the object into the air bag, about as far as it went just before it bounced. Mark the tape at the dot that was made as the object came to rest. The dots should be close together for a short interval at this point.

Now count the time that passed between the two marks you made. (You must know how rapidly dots are produced by your timer.)

4. Repeat steps 2 and 3, but this time drop the ball against a hard surface, such as the floor. Keep the height from which the object is dropped constant.

✎ a) Record how long it takes for the object to come to rest on a floor.

5. Choose two other surfaces and repeat steps 2 and 3.

✎ a) Record how long it takes the object to come to a rest each time.

✎ b) In your log, list all the surfaces you tested in the order in which you expect the most damage to be done to a falling object, to the least damage.

⚠ Set up the activity in an area clear of obstruction. Arrange for containment of the dropped object.

c) Is there a relationship between the time it takes for the object to come to rest and the potential damage to the object landing on the surface? Explain this relationship in your log.

PHYSICS TALK

Force and Impulse

Newton's First Law states that an object in motion will remain in motion unless acted upon by a force. In this activity you were able to stop an object with a force. In all cases the object was traveling at the same speed before impact. Stopping the object was done quickly or gradually. The amount of damage is related to the time during which the force stopped the object. The air bag was able to stop the object with little damage by taking a long time. The hard surface stopped the object with more damage by taking a short time.

Physicists have a useful way to describe these observations. An impulse is needed to stop an object. That impulse is defined as the product (multiplication) of the force applied and the time that the force is applied.

Impulse = $F\Delta t$

where F represents force, measured in newtons (N); Δt represents the time interval during which the force is applied, measured in seconds (s). Impulse is calculated in newton seconds (Ns).

An object of a specific mass and a specific speed will need a definite impulse to stop. Any forces acting for enough time can provide that impulse.

If the impulse required to stop is 60 Ns, a force of 60 N acting for 1 s has the required impulse. A force of 10 N acting for 6 s also has the required impulse. →

Force F	Time Interval Δt	Impulse $F\Delta t$
60 N	1 s	60 Ns
10 N	6 s	60 Ns
6000 N	0.01 s	60 Ns

The greater the force and the smaller the time interval, the greater the damage that is done.

REFLECTING ON THE ACTIVITY AND THE CHALLENGE

People once believed that the heavier the automobile, the greater the protection it offered passengers. Although a heavy, rigid car may not bend as easily as an automobile with a lighter frame, it doesn't always offer more protection.

In this activity, you found that air bags are able to protect you by extending the time it takes to stop you. Without the air bags, you will hit something and stop in a brief time. This will require a large force, large enough to injure you. With the air bag, the time to stop is longer and the force required is therefore smaller.

Force and impulse must be considered in designing your safety system. Stopping an object gradually reduces damage. The harder a surface, the shorter the stopping distance and the greater the damage. In part this provides a clue to the use of padded dashboards and sun visors in newer cars. Understanding impulse allows designers to reduce damage both to cars and passengers.

PHYSICS TO GO

1. If an impulse of 60 Ns is required to stop an object, list in your log three force and time combinations (other than those given in the Physics Talk) that can stop an object.

2. A person weighing 130 lb. (60 kg) traveling at 40 mph (18 m/s) requires an impulse of approximately 1000 Ns to stop. Calculate the force on the person if the time to stop is

   a) 0.01 s
   b) 0.1 s
   c) 1 s

3. Explain in your log why an air bag is effective. Use the terms force, impulse, and time in your response.

4. Explain in your log why a car hitting a brick wall will suffer more damage than a car hitting a snow bank.

5. There are several other safety designs that employ the concept of spreading out the time interval of a force. Describe in your log how the ones listed below perform this task:

   a) the bumper;
   b) a collapsible steering wheel;
   c) frontal "crush" zones;
   d) padding on the dashboard.

6. There are many other situations in which the force of an impulse is reduced by spreading it out over a longer time. Explain in your log how each of the actions below effectively reduces the force by increasing the time. Use the terms force, impulse, and time in your response.

   a) catching a hard ball;
   b) jumping to the ground from a height;
   c) bungee jumping;
   d) a fireman's net.

7. The speed of airplanes is considerably higher than the speed of automobiles. How might the design of a seat belt for an airplane reflect the fact that a greater impulse is exerted on a plane when it stops?

8. Airplanes have seat belts. Should they also have air bags?

Activity Five
The Rear End Collision

WHAT DO YOU THINK?

Whiplash is a serious injury that is caused by a rear-end collision. It is the focus of many lawsuits, loss of ability to work, and discomfort.

- **What is whiplash?**
- **Why is it more prominent in rear end collisions?**

Record your ideas about these questions in your *Active Physics log*. Be prepared to discuss your responses with your small group and the class.

FOR YOU TO DO

1. You will use two pieces of wood to represent the torso (the trunk of the body) and the head of a passenger. Attach a small piece of wood (about 1" x 2" x 2") to a larger piece of wood (about 1" x 3" x 10") with some duct tape acting like a hinge between the two pieces.

🖎 a) Make a sketch to show your passenger. Label what each part of the model passenger represents.

2. Set up a ramp against a stack of books about 40 cm high, as shown in the diagram below. Place the wooden model passenger at the front of a collision cart positioned about 50 cm from the end of the ramp. Release a second cart from a few centimetres up the ramp.

🖎 a) In your log record what happens to the head and torso of the wooden model.

⚠️ **Perform the activity outside of traffic areas. Do not obstruct paths to exits. Do not leave carts lying on the floor.**

3. With the first cart still positioned about 50 cm from the end of the ramp, release the second cart from the top of the ramp.

🖎 a) Describe what happens to the head of the model passenger in this collision.

🖎 b) Use Newton's First Law of Motion to explain your observations.

4. The duct tape represents the neck muscles and bones of the vertebral column. How large a force do the neck muscles exert to keep the head from flying off the body, and to return the head to the upright position? To answer this question, begin by estimating the mass of an average head.

🖎 a) Estimate and record in your log the mass of an average human head. The mass would be close to the mass of a filled water container of the same size.

TRANSPORTATION

5. Mark off a distance about 30-cm long on the lab table or the floor. Obtain a piece of wood and attach it to a spring scale. Pull the wooden mass with the spring scale over the distance you marked.

a) In your log record the force required to pull the mass and the time it took to cover the distance.

b) Repeat the step, but vary the time required to pull the mass over the distance. Record the forces and the times in your log.

c) Use your observations to complete the following statement:

The shorter the time (that is, the greater the acceleration) the ⬚ the force required.

6. The ratio of the mass of the wood to the estimated mass of the head is the same as the ratio of the forces required to pull them.

a) Use the following ratio to calculate how large a force the neck muscles exert to keep the head from flying off the body, and to return the head to the upright position under different accelerations.

$$\frac{\text{mass of head}}{\text{mass of wood}} = \frac{\text{force to move head}}{\text{force to move wood}}$$

7. Whiplash is a serious injury that can be caused by a rear-end collision. The back of the car seat pushes forward on the torso of the driver and the passengers and their bodies lunge forward. The heads remain still for a very short time. The body moving forward and the head remaining still causes the head to snap backwards. The neck muscles and bones of the vertebral column become damaged. The same muscles must then snap the head back to its place atop the shoulders.

a) What type of safety devices can reduce the delay between body and head movement to help prevent injury?

b) What additional devices have been placed in cars to help reduce the impact of rear-end collisions?

FOR YOU TO READ

Newton's Second Law of Motion

Newton's First Law of Motion is limited since it only tells you what happens to objects if no forces act upon them. Knowing that objects at rest have a tendency to remain at rest and that objects in motion will continue in motion does not provide enough information to analyze collisions. Newton's Second Law allows you to make predictions about what happens when an external force is applied to an object. If you were to place a collision cart on an even surface, it would not move. However, if you begin to push the cart, it will begin to move.

Newton's Second Law states:

If a body is acted on by a force, it will accelerate in the direction of the unbalanced force. The acceleration will be larger for smaller masses. The acceleration can be an increase in speed or a decrease in speed.

Newton's Second Law of motion indicates that the change in motion is determined by the force acting on the object, and the mass of the object itself.

REFLECTING ON THE ACTIVITY AND THE CHALLENGE

The vertebral column becomes thinner and the bones become smaller as the column attaches to the skull. The attachment bones are supported by the least amount of muscle. Unfortunately, the smaller bones, with less muscle support, make this area particularly susceptible to injury. One of the greatest dangers following whiplash is the damage to the brainstem. The brainstem is particularly vital to life support because it regulates blood pressure and breathing movements. Consider how your safety device will help prevent whiplash following a collision. What part of the restraining device prevents the movement of the head?

PHYSICS TO GO

1. Why are neck injuries common after rear-end collisions?

2. Explain why the packages in the back move forward if a truck comes to a quick stop.

3. As a bus accelerates, the passengers on the bus are jolted toward the back of the bus. Indicate what causes the passengers to be pushed backward.

4. Why would the rear-end collision demonstrated by the laboratory experiment be most dangerous for someone driving a motorcycle?

5. Would headrests serve the greatest benefit during a head-on collision or a rear-end collision? Explain your answer.

⚠ **Be sure the outside of the jar is dry so it does not slip out of your hands.**

6. A cork is attached to a string and placed in a jar of water as shown by the diagram to the right. Later, the jar is inverted.

   a) If the glass jar is pushed along the surface of a table, predict the direction in which the cork will move?

   b) If you place your left hand about 50 cm in front of the jar and push it with your right hand until it strikes your left hand, predict the direction in which the cork will move?

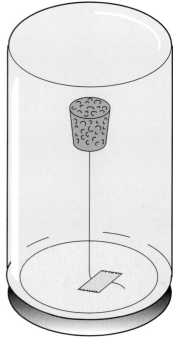

Activity Six

The Bungee Jump [Computer Analysis]

WHAT DO YOU THINK?

Bungee jumping has become a very popular sport, but it may not be for everyone. Back injuries and injuries to the ankles and hips have been associated with the sport.

- **How does a person survive a bungee jump?**
- **What would happen if an ordinary rope was used in the jump?**

Record your ideas about these questions in your *Active Physics log*. Be prepared to discuss your responses with your small group and the class.

⚠ **Set up the platform so that it is either higher or lower than eye level.**

FOR YOU TO DO

1. A force probe is connected to a computer and the concept of impulse and momentum can be used to investigate a bungee jump. Start up the force probe software and perform the probe calibrations necessary to ready the equipment for the measurement. Set the time axis for a maximum of 5 s.

2. Set up the stand and jumping platform as shown in the diagram. Attach one end of the elastic bungee cord to the foot of a small plastic doll on the jumping platform. Attach the other end of the cord to the force probe.

3. Activate the probe by clicking start. As soon as you see the line on the graph, give the plastic doll a gentle push off the platform.

   ✎ a) Use the "analyze" tool of the software to zoom in on the region corresponding to the first bounce (the spike) of the bungee jumper. Record the maximum force of the jump and the time duration.

   ✎ b) Use the software to determine the area under the spike. This is called the impulse; it is equal to the average force multiplied by the time. Record the value of the impulse.

   ✎ c) Measure the mass of the "bungee jumper" in Newtons and calculate its weight.
   Weight in Newtons (Kg. m/s^2)
   Mass in Kilograms x 9.8 m/s^2.

   ✎ d) How does the maximum force compare to the weight of the jumper?

4. Connect another type of cord to the foot of the "bungie jumper" and the force probe. Repeat step 3.

   ✎ a) Record all the measurements for a jump using this cord.

5. Use the results of your activity to answer the following questions.

a) How does the maximum force compare between the two cords?

b) How does the length of the time for the first bounce compare?

c) How does the impulse (the area under the spike) compare? What did you expect to find? Can you explain the discrepancy?

REFLECTING ON THE ACTIVITY AND CHALLENGE

The recoil from the bungee jump creates the thrill. The greater the height of the jump, the greater the recoil, and the bigger the thrill. The safety of the jump is based on increasing the stopping distance. By increasing stopping distance, the force of impact or impulse is reduced. If the jumper stopped in a very short distance the force of impact would be enormous. The bungee cord decreases the chance of injury by slowly applying a force over a much longer time to bring the jumper to rest. Use this principle in reviewing your design. What will you do to reduce the force of impact?

PHYSICS TO GO

1. Which bungee cord would you recommend for each situation below. Give your reasons.

• Cord w: long cord with little elasticity.

• Cord x: long cord with great elasticity.

• Cord y: short cord with little elasticity.

• Cord z: short cord with maximum elasticity.

a) This customer is looking for the maximum thrill. She is more concerned with speed and less concerned for safety. She is very fit and has no history of health problems.

b) This customer is looking for a thrill but is also concerned with his safety. He is looking for a little less speed and is somewhat less fit.

2. Explain why bungee jumpers of different masses often use different cords?

3. What conditions are necessary for a bungee jumper to be safe?

4. In what way can the stopping distance of the bungee jumper be related to crumple zones in automobile crashes?

5. How can momentum be used to explain why jumpers of different masses must use different bungee cords? Why can using the wrong bungee cord prove harmful to both lighter and heavier jumpers?

6. Suggest a method for determining the deceleration of the jumper during his or her descent.

7. Compare and contrast the two Force vs Time graphs shown.

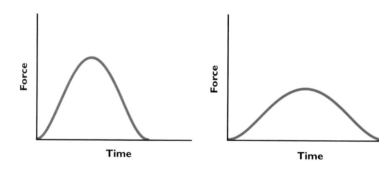

Activity Seven
Automatic Triggering Devices

WHAT DO YOU THINK?

An air bag must inflate in a sudden crash, but must not inflate under normal stopping conditions.

• How does the air bag "know" whether to inflate?

Record your ideas about these questions in your *Active Physics log*. Be prepared to discuss your responses with your small group and the class.

FOR YOU TO DO

Inquiry Investigation

1. Form engineering teams of 3-5 students. Meet with your engineering team to design an automatic air bag triggering device using a knife switch, rubber bands, string, wires, and a flashlight bulb. Other materials may also be supplied by your teacher or you.

TRANSPORTATION

Be sure to receive your teacher's approval before using any material.

2. The design parameters are as follows:

- The device must turn a flashlight bulb on, or turn it off. This will be interpreted as the trigger signal.
- The device must not trigger if the car is brought to a sudden stop from a slow speed.
- The device must trigger if the sudden stop is from a high speed.
- The car containing the device must be released down a ramp. The car will then strike a wall at the bottom of the ramp.
- The battery and bulb must be attached to the car along with the triggering device. The bulb does not have to remain in the final on or off state, but it must at least flash to show triggering.

3. Follow your teacher's guidelines for using time, space, and materials as you design your triggering device.

4. Demonstrate your design team's trigger for the class.

PHYSICS TO GO

1. How do impulse and Newton's First Law (the Law of Inertia) play a role in your air bag trigger design?

2. Imagine a device where a weight is hung from a string within a metal can. If the weight hits the side of the can, a circuit is completed. How do impulse and the Law of Inertia work in this device?

STRETCHING EXERCISES

1. How does a seat belt "know" to hold you firmly in a crash, but allow you to lean forward or adjust it without locking? Write your response in your log.

2. Go to a local auto repair shop, junk yard, or parts supply. Ask if they can show you a seat belt locking mechanism. How does it work? Construct a poster to describe what you have learned.

Activity Eight
Cushioning Collisions [Computer Analysis]

WHAT DO YOU THINK?

The use of sand canisters around bridge supports and crush zones in cars are examples of technological systems that are designed to minimize the impact of collisions between a car and a stationary object or another car.

- **How do these technological systems reduce the impact of the primary collision?**

Record your ideas about these questions in your *Active Physics log*. Be prepared to discuss your responses with your small group and the class.

FOR YOU TO DO

1. In this investigation you will be using a force probe that is attached to a computer to determine the effectiveness of different types of cushions for a toy vehicle. Release the toy car at the top of a ramp and measure the force of impact as it strikes a barrier at the bottom. A sonic ranger can be mounted on the ramp to measure the speed of the toy car prior to the collision. Open the appropriate computer files to prepare the sonic ranger to graph velocity vs. time and the force probe to graph force vs. time.

2. Mount the sonic ranger at the bottom of a ramp and place the force probe against a barrier about 10 cm from the bottom of the ramp, as shown in the diagram. Attach an index card to the back of the car, to obtain better reflection of the sound wave and improve the readings of the sonic ranger.

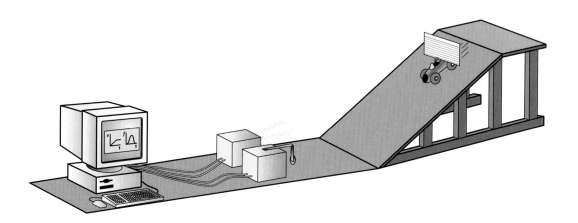

3. Conduct a few runs of the car against the force probe to ensure that the data collection equipment is working properly.

4. Attach a cushioning material to the front of the car. Conduct a number of runs with the same type of cushioning. Make sure that the car is coasting down the same slope from the same position each time.

🖊 a) Make copies of the velocity vs. time and force vs. time graphs that are displayed on the computer.

5. Repeat step 4 using other types of cushioning materials.

🖊 a) Record your observations in your log.

6. Use the graphical information you obtained in this activity to answer the following:

a) Compare the force vs. time graphs for the cushioned cars with those for the cars without cushioning.

b) Compare the areas under the force vs. time graphs for all of the experimental trials.

c) Compute the momentum of the car (the product of the mass and the velocity) prior to the collision and compare it with the area of the force vs. time graphs.

d) Summarize your comparisons in a chart.

e) How can impulse be used to explain the effectiveness of cushioning systems?

f) Describe the relationship between impulse ($F\Delta t$) and the change in momentum ($m\Delta v$).

PHYSICS TALK

Change in Momentum and Impulse

Momentum is the product of the mass and the velocity of an object.

$$p = mv$$

where p is the momentum, m is the mass, and v is the velocity.

Change in momentum is the product of mass and the change in velocity.

$$\Delta p = m\Delta v$$

Impulse = change in momentum

$$F\Delta t = m\Delta v$$

TRANSPORTATION

REFLECTING ON THE ACTIVITY AND THE CHALLENGE

What you learned in this activity better prepares you to defend the design of your safety system. The principles of momentum and impulse must be used to justify your design. Previously, you discovered objects with greater mass are more difficult to stop than smaller ones. You determined that increasing the velocity of objects also makes them more difficult to stop. Objects that have a greater mass or greater velocity have greater momentum.

Linking the two ideas together allows you to begin examining the relationship between momentum and impulse. For a large momentum change in a short time, a large force is required. A crushed rib cage or broken leg bones often result. The change in the momentum can be defined by the impulse on the object.

What devise will you use to increase the stopping time for the challenge activity? Make sure that you include impulse and change in momentum in your report. Your design features must be supported by the principles of physics.

PHYSICS TO GO

1. Helmets are designed to protect cyclists. How would the designer of helmets make use of the concept of impulse to improve their effectiveness?

2. The US Congress periodically reviews federal legislation that relates to the design of safer cars. For many years, one regulation was that car bumpers must be able to withstand a 5 mph collision. What was the intent of this regulation? The speed was later lowered to 3 mph. Why? Should it be changed again?

3. If a car has a mass of 1200 kg and an initial velocity of 10 m/s (about 20 mph) calculate the change in momentum required to:

   a) bring it to rest
   b) slow it to 5 m/s (approximately 10 mph)

4. If the braking force for a car is 10,000 N, calculate the impulse if the brake is applied for 1.2 s. If the car has a mass of 1200 kg, what is the change in velocity of the car over this 1.2 s time interval?

5. A 1500 kg car, traveling at 5 m/s after braking, strikes a power pole and comes to a full stop in 0.1 s. Calculate the force exerted by the power pole and brakes required to stop the car.

6. For the car described in question 5, explain why a break-away pole that brings the car to rest after 2.8 s is safer than the conventional power pole?

7. Write a short essay relating your explanation for the operation of the cushioning systems to the explanation of the operation of the air bags.

8. Explain why a collapsible steering wheel is able to help prevent injuries during a car crash.

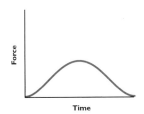

9. Compare and contrast the two Force vs Time graphs shown.

STRETCHING EXERCISE

Package an egg in a small container so that the egg will not break upon impact. Your teacher will provide the limitations in the construction of your package. You may be limited to two pieces of paper and some tape. You may be limited to a certain size package or a package of a certain weight. Bring your package to class so that it can be compared in a crash test with the other packages.

(HINT: Place each egg in a plastic bag before packaging to help avoid a messy cleanup.)

Activity Nine
Safety in the Air

WHAT DO YOU THINK?

The excitement of your first plane ride has continued to build and you are not even off the ground. You begin to wonder if that person seated by the exit door is capable of carrying out the responsibilities that the flight attendant has just described.

- **What do you think should be the requirements for sitting in an exit row?**
- **If you were limited to three requirements, what would they be?**

Record your ideas about these questions in your *Active Physics log*. Be prepared to discuss your responses with your small group and the class.

FOR YOU TO DO

1. On the following pages is the safety information of an airline. Read it carefully.

a) Write down your interpretations of the requirements for sitting in an exit seat.

 *IT'S ON TIME* **AIRLINES**

Exit Seating

The Federal Aviation Administration (FAA) regulations (14CFR, part 121) outline specific policies and procedures U.S. air carriers must follow concerning exit seating in aircraft. The following content of the rules is being provided for your information and guidance.

RESTRICTIONS

No air carrier may seat a person in a designated exit seat if it is likely that the person would be unable to perform one or more of the applicable functions listed under REQUIREMENTS below because—

1. The person lacks sufficient mobility, strength, or dexterity in both arms and hands, and both legs to
   (A) reach upward, sideways, and downward to the location of emergency exit and exit slide operating mechanismisms;
   (B) grasp and push, pull, turn, or otherwise manipulate those mechanisms;
   (C) push, shove, pull or otherwise open emergency exits;
   (D) lift out, hold, deposit on nearby seats, or maneuver over the seatbacks to the next row objects the size and weight of over-wing window exit doors (approximately 24 1/4"x 39" and up to 53 lbs);
   (E) remove obstructions similar in size and weight to over-wing exit doors (approximately 24 1/4" x 39" and up to 53 lbs);
   (F) reach the emergency exit expeditiously;
   (G) maintain balance while removing obstructions;
   (H) exit expeditiously;
   (I) stabilize an escape slide after deployment, or
   (J) assist others in getting of an escape slide, or
2. The person is less than 15 years of age, or
3. The person lacks the capacity to perform one or more of the applicable functions without the assistance of an adult companion, parent, or other relative, or
4. The persons lacks the ability to read and understand instructions related to emergency evacuation provided by the air carrier in printed or graphic form or the ability to understand oral crew commands, or
5. The person lacks sufficient visual capacity to perform one or more of the applicable functions without the assistance of visual aids beyond contact lenses or eyeglasses or
6. The person lacks sufficient aural capacity to hear and understand instructions shouted by crew members without assistance beyond a hearing aid, or
7. The person lacks the ability to convey information orally to other passengers, or
8. The person has (a) a condition or responsibilities, such as caring for small children that might prevent the person from performing one or more of the applicable functions or (b) a condition that might cause the person harm if he or she performs one or more of the applicable functions.

→

REQUIREMENTS FOR SITTING IN EXIT SEATS

In the event of an emergency in which a crew member is not available to assist in an evacuation of the aircraft a passenger occupying an exit seat may be asked to perform the following functions:

1. Locate the emergency exit;
2. Recognize the emergency exit opening mechanism;
3. Comprehend the instructions for operating the emergency exits;
4. Operate the emergency exit;
5. Assess whether opening the emergency exit will increase the hazards to which passengers may be exposed;
6. Follow oral directions and hand signals given by crew member;
7. Stow or secure the emergency exit door so that it will not impede use of the exit;
8. Assess the condition of an escape slide, activate the slide, and stabilize the slide after deployment to assist others in getting off the slide;
9. Pass expeditiously through the emergency exit; and
10. Assess, select, and follow a safe path away from the emergency exit and aircraft.

Any passengers assigned an exit seat may request reseating if they:

1. Cannot meet the selection criteria above:
2. Have a nondiscernible condition that will prevent them from performing the applicable functions.
3. May suffer bodily harm as a result of performing one or more of the applicable functions;
4. Do not wish to perform these functions.

If you would like to change your seat for a non-exit seat, please see the It's on time agent or flight attendant. U.S. government regulations prohibit an individual from sitting in a designated exit seat if they cannot speak, read or understand the instructions.

Your understanding and compliance with these FAA regulations will be appreciated.

Thank you.

2. Meet with your design team to develop a test that could be used at the airport check-in counter to determine a person's fitness for an exit-door seat. Your test will be applied to a person from outside your group. Be ready to defend the reasons behind your test.

   Consider some of the following questions in designing your test and in evaluating the tests of other groups:

   • Does the test cover all essential requirements?
   • Does the test provide essential information?
   • Does the test address communications skills?
   • Is the test quick?
   • Does the test avoid embarrassment?
   • Is the test necessary?

PHYSICS TO GO

1. The Exit Seating Instruction Sheet is long and complicated. Rewrite it in simpler words on a 5" x 8" card that could be glued to the seat back.

2. Does the Exit Seating Instruction Sheet convey the right information? Translate the English version into another language that you speak or study.

3. What additional requirements might you include on the Exit Seating Instruction Sheet?

4. Look up the statistics concerning accidents. Compare the numbers for the airline industry with those of the automotive industry. Which is a safer means of transportation? Safety is often described in terms of deaths per thousand passenger-miles. Is that a good measure? Is it appropriate for comparing passenger cars to planes? What about other means of mass transit: planes, trains and school buses?

5. Write an Exit Seating Instruction Sheet for a train.

6. Write an Exit Seating Instruction Sheet for a school bus.

7. How would you get the passengers to pay attention to the emergency instructions given by flight attendants at the beginning of each flight?

PHYSICS
AT WORK

Mohan Thomas

DESIGNING AUTOMOBILES
THAT SAVE LIVES

Mo is a Senior Project Engineer at General Motors North American Operation's (NAO) Safety Center and his responsibilities include making sure that different General Motors vehicles meet national safety requirements. Several of the design features that Mo has helped to develop have been implemented into vehicles that are now out on the road.

"This is how it works," he explains. "An engineer for a vehicle comes to us here at the Safety Center and requests technical assistance with design features to help them meet the side impact crash regulations required by the government. You have to analyze the physical forces of an event, which involves one car hitting another car on the side and then the door smashing into the driver," he continues. "We'll study the velocity, acceleration, momentum, and inertia in an event, as well as the materials used in the vehicle itself."

"The initial energy of an impact from one vehicle on another," states Mo, " has to be managed by the vehicle that's getting hit. Our goal is to manage the energy in such a way that the occupant in the vehicle being hit is protected. You take the forces that are coming into the vehicle and you redirect them into areas around the occupant. The frame work of the car, therefore, is very important to the design, as well as energy absorbing materials used in the vehicle."

Mo grew up in Chicago, Illinois, and has always enjoyed math and science, but he was also interested in creative writing. He wanted to combine math and science with creative work and has found that combination in the design work of engineering. "The nice part of being at the Safety Center," states Mo, "is that you know that you are contributing to something meaningful. The bottom line is that the formulas and problems that we are working on are meant to save people's lives."

Chapter 2 Assessment

Your design team will develop a safety system for protecting automobile, airplane, bicycle, motorcycle or train passengers. As you study existing safety systems, you and your design team should be listing ideas for improving an existing system or designing a new system for preventing accidents. You may also consider a system that will minimize the harm caused by accidents.

Your final product will be a working model or prototype of a safety system. On the day that you bring the final product to class, the teams will display them around the room while class members informally view them and discuss them with members of the design team. At this time, class members will generate questions about each others' products. The questions will be placed in envelopes provided to each team by the teacher. The teacher will use some of these questions during the oral presentations on the next day. The product will be judged according to the following:

1. The quality of your safety feature enhancement and the working model or prototype.

2. The quality of a 5-minute oral report that should include:

- **the need for the system;**
- **the method used to develop the working model;**
- **demonstration of the working model;**
- **discussion of the physics concepts involved;**
- **description of the next-generation version of the system;**
- **answers to questions posed by the class.**

3. The quality of a written and/or multimedia report including:

- **the information from the oral report;**
- **documentation of the sources of expert information;**
- **discussion of consumer acceptance and market potential;**
- **discussion of the physics concepts applied in the design of the safety system.**

Criteria

Review the criteria that were agreed to at the beginning of the chapter. If they require modification, come to an agreement with the teacher and the class.

Your project should be judged by you and your design team according to the criteria before you display and share it with your class. Being able to judge the quality of your own work before you submit it is one of the skills that will make you a "treasured employee"!

Physics You Learned

Newton's First Law of Motion (inertia)

Pressure (N/m^2)

Pressure = $\dfrac{\text{force}}{\text{area}}$ $(P = \dfrac{F}{a})$

Distance vs time relationships

Time interval =
$\quad$ time$_{(final)}$ − time$_{(initial)}$ $(\Delta t = t_f - t_i)$

Impulse (N × *time*),

Impulse =
$\quad$ force × time interval (Impulse = $F \times \Delta t$)

Stopping distance

Newton's Second Law of Motion, constant
$\quad$ acceleration, force
$\quad$ Force = mass × acceleration
$\qquad$ $F = ma$

Momentum = mass × velocity ($p = mv$)

Conservation of momentum

Change in momentum is affected by mass
and change in velocity

Change in momentum =
$\quad$ mass × change in velocity ($\Delta p = m\, \Delta v$)

Impulse =
$\quad$ change in momentum ($F\, \Delta t = m\, \Delta v$)

JOURNEY TO THE MOON AND BEYOND

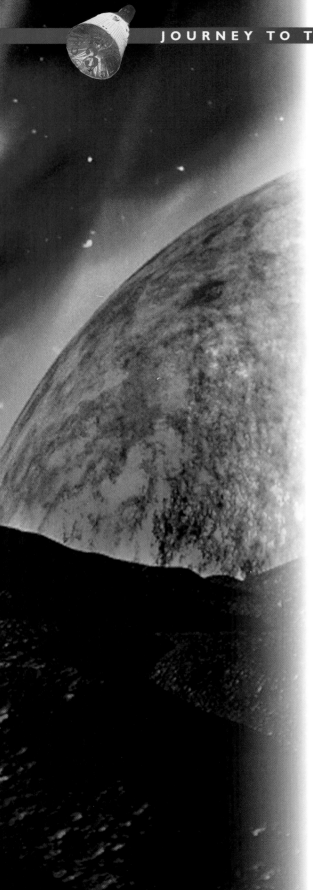

Scenario

"Do you know what life is like with a science fiction addict in the house? It is not easy. My little brother thinks our house is a colony on Mars, our garage is a space station, and our car is a star ship. You wouldn't believe the roles that I have had to play just to get some peace and quiet. It's a good thing that my Mom and Dad are good sports, scheduling launch opportunities, spacewalks, and nourishment periods. If you beam over to our place, be sure to refer to the microwave oven as a food replicator. Sometimes it is fun, like when he calls our grumpy, old cat a hostile alien. But it can be rough when he has trouble telling the difference between science fact and science fiction."

Challenge

Science fiction is a very popular style of writing. The bookstores and libraries are filled with science fiction literature. Some of the books and movies such as *Frankenstein*, *2001 – A Space Odyssey*, *Jurassic Park*, *Dr. Jekyll and Mr. Hyde*, *E.T.*, and *Star Wars* have become classics. Not only are the writers of these books or scripts creative writers with wonderful imaginations, but also they are all very knowledgeable about science. It is not uncommon for a science fiction writer or film director to consult with scientists to ensure that the ideas they use are credible. Can you imagine writing a script for a blockbuster, science-fiction movie? If you are successful, you provide entertainment for millions of people and earn lots of money! Some science-fiction movies have even gone beyond entertainment and provided ideas for scientists to develop. To write effectively, you must have good ideas and you must have an accurate understanding of your subject.

Criteria

You should discuss the criteria for this challenge in your small groups and then with the whole class. For instance, you should discuss:

- **the maximum and minimum length of the story and annotation;**
- **how much of the grade should depend on creativity and interest in the story;**
- **how much should depend on the annotation that relates and describes the real physics in your story and your modifications of physics;**
- **how many physics concepts you should include to receive an "A" for your work.**

Generate criteria that the class can all agree on. Be as specific as possible. A clear understanding of how your project will be graded will make it easier to do the best job possible.

Your challenge is to help my little brother, or any other young sci-fi fan, learn the difference between science fact and science fiction.

- **Write a science fiction story that incorporates a trip to the moon or beyond.**
- **In a separate key to your story (an annotation), you must explain where the science is true and where you have modified the physics for interest or excitement.**

Activity One

Weight Change during Takeoff

WHAT DO YOU THINK?

You are standing on a scale in an elevator on the ground floor. The elevator starts moving up abruptly.

• What happens to the weight reading on the scale?

Record your ideas about this question in your *Active Physics log*. Be prepared to discuss your responses with your small group and the class.

FOR YOU TO DO

1. Anyone who has ever ridden in an elevator has felt as though his or her weight is changing. Depending on how the elevator is moving, you may feel suddenly lighter or heavier. Close your eyes and imagine you are in an elevator.

🔖 a) As the elevator starts to rise, what seems to happen to your weight?

🔖 b) As the elevator is about to stop on your floor, what seems to happen to your weight?

2. The effective change in your weight can be measured. Look at the video recording of someone standing on a bathroom scale inside an elevator. (You may want to make your own video to compare the changes in the scale reading with those on the video.)

🔖 Record, in your log, the scale readings of weight at five different moments:
   a) when the elevator is at rest;
   b) when it starts to rise;
   c) when it is rising at a constant speed;
   d) when it starts to descend from the top;
   e) when it is going down at a constant speed.

⚠ **Make sure the kilogram mass is securely attached to the spring scale.**

3. Make a model of the elevator, in the form of a small box. Fasten a spring scale inside the top of the box to represent the bathroom scale. Instead of a person, suspend a kilogram mass from the scale. With the model elevator at rest on earth, observe the reading on the spring scale.

🔖 a) What is the reading on the spring scale? What are the units of force?

! **Do not raise the box above the level of your head. Keep all motion away from the plane of your body.**

! **Do not lift the box so quickly that the kilogram mass becomes unstable.**

4. Lift the elevator gradually, moving it up at a constant speed, and then stop it.

a) During this journey of the "elevator," record in your log the changes in the reading of the spring scale.

5. Repeat the movement of the elevator, but start the elevator at the top and have it go down.

a) Record the changes in the reading of the spring scale in your log.

6. Continue to move the elevator with different accelerations, both up and down, until you feel confident that you know when a scale value does change and when it doesn't change.

a) Look at the measurements you obtained and generalize the results in your log.

b) Under what conditions does the person in the elevator experience a change of weight? (Try to explain using the terms *velocity* and *acceleration.*)

c) Under what conditions is the apparent weight (the weight the scale reads) greater than the "person's" normal weight?

d) Under what conditions is the apparent weight smaller?

PHYSICS TALK

Velocity is speed with direction, for example, 30 m/s south, or 25 m/s up. Acceleration is defined as a change in velocity over time. Most people think of acceleration as a change in speed. However, acceleration can also be a change in direction.

FOR YOU TO READ
Newton's Explanation of Gravity

You know that things fall to the ground because of gravity. More than 300 years ago, Sir Isaac Newton described gravity as a universal force. Gravity is the force that tends to attract any two masses. Since planets are such big masses, gravity tends to pull objects towards the center of the Earth, moon, or other planets.

Newton recognized that gravity extends beyond Earth. According to Newton's First Law of Motion, objects in motion should continue in motion, in a straight line at a constant speed, unless they are acted upon by some force. But Newton, as others before him, noted that the planets do not travel in straight lines. As early as the time of the ancient Greek philosopher Aristotle, scientists knew that planets orbit in a curved pathway. Newton reasoned that some force must act upon the planets that prevents them from moving in a straight line. He concluded that the force must be the same force of gravity as found on Earth.

According to Newton, every mass in the universe attracts every other mass. The attraction between the masses is proportional to the size of the masses and inversely proportional to the distance between them. That means that the gravitational attraction increases as the mass of objects gets larger. In part, that explains why you would have greater weight on Jupiter than planet Earth. Jupiter has a greater mass than planet Earth and exerts a greater gravitational force. Gravity is so strong on Jupiter (more than 2.5 times as great as Earth) that your legs may not be able to support you. If you weigh 150 lbs. on Earth, you would weigh 380 lbs. on Jupiter. The second part of the relation indicates that the gravitational force decreases as the distance between the objects increases. While traveling far from Earth, you will weigh less owing to this distance change.

How does change in gravity relate to the observations you made in this activity? There are two equivalent ways of describing what happens in an elevator when a scale reading changes. You can account for the scale reading as a "change in weight of the passenger" due to the acceleration of the elevator. You can also account for the scale reading as a "change in gravity within the elevator." If you didn't know that you were in an elevator, there would be no way to determine if the weight change was due to the elevator's acceleration or to a change in gravity. This is one of the ideas in Einstein's Theory of General Relativity!

REFLECTING ON THE ACTIVITY AND THE CHALLENGE

In constructing your science fiction story, think about why an understanding of gravity is important to your story line. You know that the weight of a body or a 1-kg mass changes as a result of the acceleration of the elevator.

Your science fiction story may include a blast-off or a landing sequence. During take-off there is a large acceleration and the occupants in the vehicle will feel much heavier, as you determined in the elevator experiments. How would you describe this in an interesting manner to the readers of your story?

In the old Mercury rocket ships, the acceleration at liftoff was so great that the crew had to wear special pressurized suits and lie down in special couches when the ship took off. In a rising elevator, you might feel your stomach being left behind. In a Mercury liftoff, there was a real danger of internal injury.

Landing on a new planet may also include some descriptions of the lower or higher gravity that you find there. If there is a very large gravity, walking and running will be quite difficult. While traveling through space, you may weigh very little in the capsule because you are so distant from any planet. Including good physics with an interesting story line is your challenge for this chapter.

PHYSICS TO GO

1. Take a spring scale and a 1-kg mass into an elevator. (Better yet, stand on a bathroom scale in the elevator.) Be sure to ask the building manager for permission to use the elevator. Hold the spring scale as steady as possible. Record the values of the spring scale or the bathroom scale as the elevator starts, stops, and moves up between floors. Repeat the measurements for the elevator going down.

2. A 1-kg mass weighs 9.8 N when the elevator is at rest. You can measure the acceleration of the elevator by noting the value of the spring scale on the ascent. Each 9.8 N is 1 Earth gravity which is also referred to as "1g". If the spring scale reads 9.8 N, this is "1g" (gravity on Earth). If the spring scale reads 2×9.8 N = 19.6 N, this is "2g" (gravity on Earth + acceleration equal to the Earth's gravity.)

   a) What is the acceleration if the scale reads 29.4 N ("3g")?
   b) What is the acceleration if the scale reads 14.7 N ("1.5g")?
   c) What is the acceleration if the scale reads 24.5 N?
   d) What was the acceleration of the elevator you tested?

3. A bathroom scale measures your weight by recording the compression of a spring. When you stand on the scale and the elevator is not accelerating, the spring compresses enough to support you. This reading is your weight. When the elevator accelerates up, the spring must compress more in order to both support you and accelerate you up. Explain why the scale reading is less when the elevator accelerates down.

4. During an automobile crash, a car's acceleration was measured as 50 m/s^2 ("5g"). A 10-kg baby would have an apparent weight of five times his/her normal weight. What significance does this have for child safety?

5. Calculate the weight of a person weighing 120 lb. on Earth if they were on:

   a) Jupiter where gravitational attraction is 2.5 times greater than that of Earth.
   b) Mars where gravitational attraction is only $\frac{1}{3}$ that of Earth.
   c) The moon where gravitational attraction is 16% that of planet Earth.

6. Use the diagram below to help explain the following questions.

   a) Explain why the weight of the astronaut changes as he moves away from the planet's surface?

   b) Would it take greatest force to move the astronaut from the planet if he were found in: position A, position B, or position C? Explain your answer.

   c) Find the weight of the astronaut at positions which are (4×6400) km, (5×6400) km, and (6×6400) km from the center of the planet. Graph the weight vs these positions.

   d) How would life in a spacecraft change as it moves away from Earth.

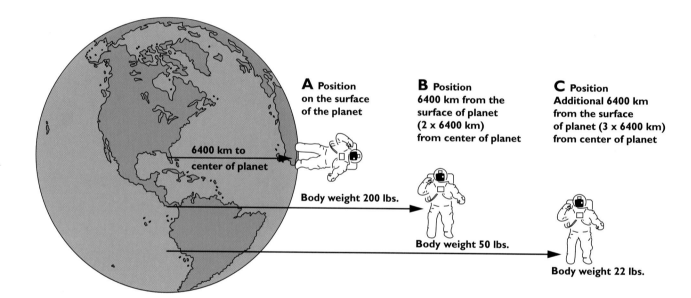

7. Compare the force required (and the amount of fuel needed) to launch a spaceship from:

   a) planet Earth and the moon (Which has $\frac{1}{6}$ of Earth's gravity).

   b) planet Earth and Jupiter (Which has 2.5 times Earth's gravity).

STRETCHING EXERCISES

1. Place an object in a small box to represent a person in an elevator. Attach the box to a force probe connected to a computer. You can either connect the box on top of the probe or suspend it by a string from the bottom. The results will be the same.

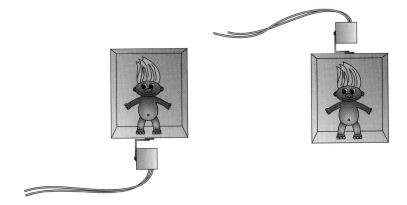

2. Hold the probe stationary and activate the software. The probe will be measuring the weight of the object and box. Start the force probe up and try to maintain a constant velocity. Explain the resulting graph.

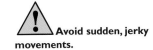 **Avoid sudden, jerky movements.**

3. Hold the force probe with the box about 5 feet above the floor and activate the software. Start the force probe down and try to maintain a constant velocity. Explain the resulting graph.

4. Repeat the last part of the experiment; this time, however, start the force probe down faster. You should notice that the dip in the graph is closer to zero. Under what conditions would the graph reach zero force?

5. Compare the results of the computer testing of the elevator with the videotape experiment.

Activity Two
Weightlessness with Gravity

WHAT DO YOU THINK?

When you watch the astronauts in the space shuttle orbiting the Earth, they appear weightless.

• **Draw a picture which includes Earth and the moon to scale. Place the space shuttle at one point in its orbit between Earth and the moon.**

• **Why do astronauts appear weightless in the space shuttle?**

Record your ideas about these questions in your *Active Physics log*. Be prepared to discuss your responses with your small group and the class.

FOR YOU TO DO

1. Take a Styrofoam cup and use a pen to punch two small holes on opposite sides of the cup near the bottom. Fill the cup with water while keeping the holes closed with two fingers. Carefully stand on a table and release the cup so that it lands in a garbage pail near the floor.

✎a) In your log record what you observe as the cup is in free fall.

✎b) Provide an explanation for your observations.

2. Make a small hole in the bottom of a Styrofoam cup and position a paper clip outside of the cup. Attach two elastic bands to the paper clip, as shown in the diagram, and then attach metal washers to the opposite end of the elastic bands. Stretch the rubber bands slightly so that the washers hang just below the surface of the cup.

⚠ **Immediately clean up any spilled water.**

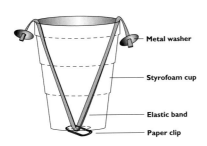

Metal washer
Styrofoam cup
Elastic band
Paper clip

✎a) Predict what will happen if the cup is dropped.
✎b) Provide an explanation for your predictions.
✎c) Drop the cup and observe it in free fall. Record your observations in your log.
✎d) Provide an explanation for your observations.

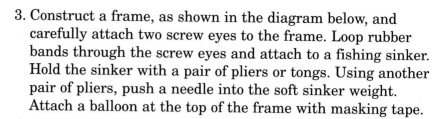

If any lead dust is created by boring or abrasion, carefully clean it up. Wash your hands.

3. Construct a frame, as shown in the diagram below, and carefully attach two screw eyes to the frame. Loop rubber bands through the screw eyes and attach to a fishing sinker. Hold the sinker with a pair of pliers or tongs. Using another pair of pliers, push a needle into the soft sinker weight. Attach a balloon at the top of the frame with masking tape.

a) Predict what will happen if the frame is dropped.

b) Provide an explanation for your predictions.

c) Drop the metal frame and observe it during free fall. Record your observations in your log.

d) Provide an explanation for your observations.

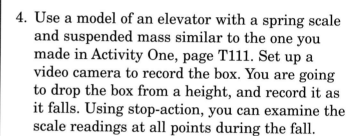

4. Use a model of an elevator with a spring scale and suspended mass similar to the one you made in Activity One, page T111. Set up a video camera to record the box. You are going to drop the box from a height, and record it as it falls. Using stop-action, you can examine the scale readings at all points during the fall.

a) What does the scale read while the box is in free fall?

Here are some possibilities:
• It reads 9.8 N throughout.
• It starts at 9.8 N and decreases as it falls.
• It reads zero throughout the fall.
• It starts at 9.8 N and increases.
• It starts at zero and increases.

5. Repeat the experiment of the box falling. This time push the box off the table so that it moves horizontally as it falls.

a) Write the results of this experiment in your log.

FOR YOU TO READ

What is Free Fall?

When the "elevator" box is falling freely, the only force acting on it is gravity, and yet there is no apparent gravity inside the box (the weight is zero). This was the situation when the box was dropped. It was also what happened when the box was shoved horizontally. It does not matter which way the box is moving. As long as the only force acting on the box is gravity, it is in free fall, and gravity seems to disappear inside it.

When a skydiver is falling to the Earth, the only force acting on her is gravity. Does she appear weightless? If she were falling and she dropped a pencil, the pencil would also fall. The pencil would fall as fast as she would. As far as she is concerned, the pencil would be hovering in front of her in midair—the pencil would be weightless.

In the space shuttle, the astronauts are falling to the Earth for days and days. During the time of their fall, they appear to be weightless. The space shuttle orbits the Earth at a height of only 250 km or 150 miles. There is plenty of gravity. But since the only force acting on the space shuttle and the astronauts is gravity (they are falling to the Earth), they appear weightless.

How can something be falling to the Earth (and be weightless) and yet not hit the Earth? Imagine a cannon atop a very high mountain as shown in the diagram. If the cannon shoots a ball horizontally with a small speed, the cannon may land just past the mountain. If the ball is shot with a greater speed, it will land further away from the mountain. If the speed of the ball is greater still, it may fall towards the Earth, but the curvature of the Earth keeps the ball from landing. The ball will continue to fall, but the Earth's curvature keeps the ball above the ground. The space shuttle is falling toward the Earth (and all of the astronauts are weightless) but the space shuttle does not hit the Earth because of its horizontal velocity. It is like the cannon ball shot from the high mountain with a large speed. The diagram shows the path of cannonballs shot from an imaginary high mountain. It also shows orbits that other satellites would have if they could be shot horizontally from even higher mountains. Does it surprise you that the picture was drawn by Isaac Newton in the early 1700s, long before anyone seriously considered space travel? Newton's genius was not that he saw the apple fall from the tree and hit the ground. It was that he imagined the moon also falling, even though he knew the moon would never hit the ground.

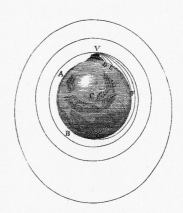

REFLECTING ON THE ACTIVITY OR CHALLENGE

The longer the spaceflight between Earth and the moon (or beyond), the greater the number of problems faced by the astronauts. As the spacecraft orbits the new planet, weight appears to have disappeared. An analogy can be drawn between a skydiver who drops a pencil while falling to the Earth and the astronaut aboard the spacecraft. The pencil, dropped by the skydiver, appears to float because it falls at the same speed as the skydiver. The pencil would appear to be weightless. As the spacecraft orbits the planet, the astronauts also appear to be weightless. Although gravity still exists, the spacecraft and astronaut are in free fall. Objects float about the spacecraft, much like the pencil would float about for the skydiver.

The feeling of weightlessness presents special difficulties. Many everyday tasks must be rethought. Consider how difficult in would be to pour a glass of milk or the difficulties you would experience going to the bathroom. What kinds of problems are experienced in a weightless environment? What parts of your story can be challenged?

PHYSICS TO GO

1. A scale drawing will show how close the shuttle is to the surface of the Earth. The radius of the Earth is 6400 km (4000 miles). The shuttle orbits at a height of 250 km (150 miles). Draw a scale model showing the size of the Earth and the space shuttle's position relative to it.

2. If a 70-kg astronaut inside a space craft orbiting the Earth at an altitude of 130 miles steps on a bathroom scale, explain why the scale will read zero?

3. Interview five people you know well. Ask them why they think the astronauts appear weightless when they are in the space shuttle. If any of them think it is because there is no gravity there, try to help them change their misconceptions. Use the results of your experiment to help convince them. (This is tough, people do not like to change their minds.)

4. Carefully examine the picture of the elevator. If the elevator were in free fall, predict the direction that the balloon and the anvil will move once they are released. Provide an explanation for your prediction.

5. Have you ever hit an air pocket while on board an airplane, and experienced the plane drop? Compare the sensation of hitting a down draft to the way that astronauts feel in a weightless environment.

6. Airplanes can achieve low gravity for periods of 25 s. In Houston, the Johnson Space Center operates a KC-135 aircraft, called the "vomit comet," for astronaut training. The jet is a Boeing 707 with most of the seats removed and padded walls to protect the people inside of the plane. The plane travels in a parabolic flight pattern, first it climbs at a 45° angle, levels off, and then descends at the same 45° angle, before pulling out of the dive, as shown in the diagram. During the flight it ranges in altitude from 7.3 km to 10.4 km.

   a) If a person stood on a scale, indicate which points A,B,C, D, or E would show greatest weight. Explain your answer.
   b) In which part of the flight would the person experience weightlessness? Explain your answer.

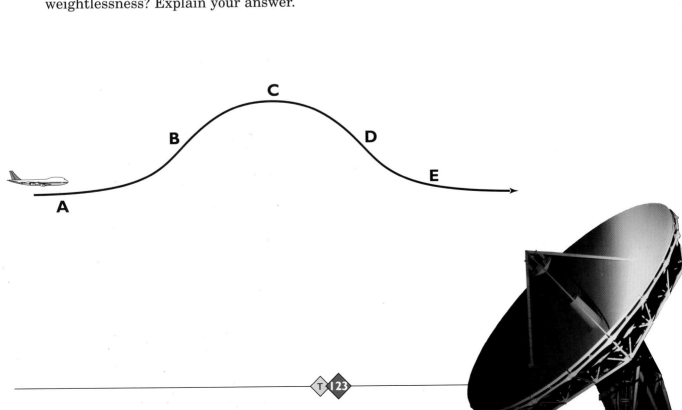

Activity Three

Spreadsheet Games: Free Fall

WHAT DO YOU THINK?

Almost 400 years ago, Galileo performed an experiment in which he dropped two objects of different weights off a high tower.

• **Which one do you think hit the ground first?**

• **Would objects fall differently on the moon and Jupiter than on Earth?**

Record your ideas about these questions in your *Active Physics log*. Be prepared to discuss your responses with your small group and the class.

FOR YOU TO DO

In this activity you will use spreadsheets to experiment with what happens during free fall. You can use the copies of the spreadsheets shown in the text, or enter your own data into the spreadsheet program provided by your teacher. The spreadsheet file will enable you to calculate distance, velocity, and acceleration for an object in free fall. The first page of the spreadsheet consists of a set of initial conditions that you can change, along with a units converter. The second page graphs the information. The third page consists of long columns where the values of time, velocity, acceleration, and distance are calculated.

The initial conditions for the problem are the mass of the object that is falling, the acceleration due to gravity and the drag factor. The drag factor is a constant that is used to calculate the value of air resistance on the object.

time	accel	ave vel	new acc	dist fallen	velocity
0.30	9.80	2.45	9.80	0.44	2.94
0.40	9.80	3.43	9.80	0.78	3.92
0.50	9.80	4.41	9.80	1.23	4.90
0.60	9.80	5.39	9.80	1.76	5.88
0.70	9.80	6.37	9.80	2.40	6.86
0.80	9.80	7.35	9.80	3.14	7.84
0.90	9.80	8.33	9.80	3.97	8.82
1.00	9.80	9.31	9.80	4.90	9.80
1.10	9.80	10.29	9.80	5.93	10.78
1.20	9.80	11.27	9.80	7.06	11.76
1.30	9.80	12.25	9.80	8.28	12.74
1.40	9.80	13.23	9.80	9.60	13.72
1.50	9.80	14.21	9.80	11.03	14.70
1.60	9.80	15.19	9.80	12.54	15.68
1.70	9.80	16.17	9.80	14.16	16.66
1.80	9.80	17.15	9.80	15.88	17.64
1.90	9.80	18.13	9.80	17.69	18.62

Note: To enter a number in the spreadsheet, click in the box, type the number (do not include units or commas) and press **enter** . *If you get the message, "Locked cells cannot be changed," it means that you did not click in the proper box. Try again.*

On the next pages are a few problems for you to examine with the spreadsheet. The power of the computer spreadsheet is that it allows you to see very quickly the physics in each problem without having to spend time on tedious calculations. By just changing the initial conditions you will be able to see instantly both the numerical and graphical results of those changes.

Problem 1: Throwing a Penny off the Empire State Building

If you throw a penny off the Empire State Building, how fast will it be traveling when it strikes the sidewalk?

1. Look at the copies of graphs shown.

✎a) What is the approximate height of the Empire State Building in meters?

2. Enter the following initial conditions on the spreadsheet:

Acceleration   9.800 | enter |

Drag factor   0.000 | enter | (assume no air resistance)

Mass   0.003 | enter | (mass of a penny is about 0.003 kg)

Active Physics: Spreadsheet Games

MASS OF FALLING OBJECT

> 0.003
> Kgm

ACCELERATION (g)

> 9.8
> m/s^2

DRAG FACTOR

> 0

CONVERSION FACTORS

distance in feet

> 1000
> feet

distance in meters

> 304.8
> meters

velocity in m/s

>
> m/s

velocity in mph

> 0.000
> mph

3. At the bottom of the spreadsheet are labeled tabs. Click the tab labeled GRAPHS. Sketch the graphs for velocity vs. distance, velocity vs. time, distance vs. time, and acceleration vs. time. You will have to scroll the spreadsheet to see all the graphs.

✎a) Look at the velocity vs. distance graph to see how fast the penny was traveling when it traveled a distance equivalent to the height of the Empire State Building.

✎b) How fast is this is in miles per hour? (Use the converter on the spreadsheet program or a conversion calculator.)

✎c) Do you think that this is the real velocity of a penny when it reaches the sidewalk?

✎d) What factors do you think would cause the penny to move slower?

4. In reality, there is air resistance on the penny as it falls. Take this air resistance into account. An approximate value for the drag factor for the penny is $0.0001 \text{ Ns}^2/\text{m}^2$. Enter this value of the drag factor in the box on the CALCULATION spreadsheet and press `enter` .

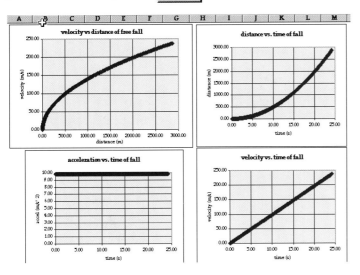

5. Switch to the GRAPHS spreadsheet and again sketch the graphs that you see.

a) Discuss how the graphs differ from those for the no air resistance case.

b) What is the maximum speed attained by the penny when air resistance is taken into account?

c) Does the penny reach terminal velocity by the time it hits the sidewalk?

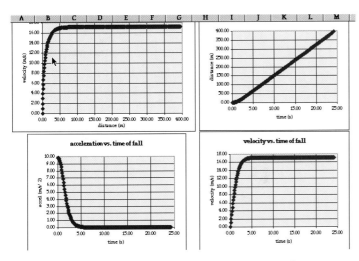

TRANSPORTATION

Problem 2: The Falling Human Problem

Occasionally you read what seem to be completely ridiculous stories in the supermarket tabloids. One such story might have the headline, "Man Falls from Airplane and Survives!" Is this headline believable? How fast would a person be going when he hits the ground? If the answer is 10 miles per hour, is the story reasonable? What if the answer were about 60, 100, or 1000 miles per hour when the person hits the ground?

1. Use the spreadsheet to determine how fast a person is traveling when he hits the ground. An approximate value of the drag factor for a human is $0.2 \text{ Ns}^2/\text{m}^2$. Enter the following initial conditions on the spreadsheet:

Acceleration 9.800 | enter |

Drag factor   0.2 | enter |

Mass   60.0 | enter | (approximate mass of a person = 60 kg)

2. Sketch the graphs.

a) Do the graphs differ from the penny with air resistance? If so, explain the difference.

3. Now assume the plane is flying at an altitude of 3600 feet. You are going to use the spreadsheet to see how fast the person is moving when he has fallen a distance of 3600 feet.

a) Use the converter to determine how many meters is equal to 3600 feet.

b) What is the velocity in meters per second when the person has fallen 3600 feet?

c) Use the converter to determine the velocity in miles per hour.

d) Do you think the headline is possible? Discuss your answer.

Problem 3: Parachute Problem

A simple change to the spreadsheet will allow you to examine what happens in a situation in which a person "falls" out of an airplane with a parachute. An approximate value of the drag factor for a parachute is 20 Ns^2/m^2.

1. Enter the following initial conditions on the spreadsheet:

Acceleration 9.8   **enter**

Drag factor   20.0   **enter**

Mass   60.0   **enter**   (approximate mass of a
                        person = 60 kg)

🖘a) Note how quickly terminal velocity is reached.

🖘b) Why is this not a completely accurate representation of a
    person jumping with a parachute?

Problem 4 : Free Fall on Other Planets

Compare what happens on Earth with what happens in a smaller gravitational field such as the moon's, and a larger gravitational field such as Jupiter's.

1. Examine a falling 1 kg ball on Earth. Ignore air resistance for this part of the activity. Enter the following initial conditions on the spreadsheet.

Acceleration 9.8   **enter**

Drag factor   0.0   **enter**

Mass   1.0   **enter**

🖘a) How fast is the ball moving after 1 s?

🖘b) How far did the ball fall in 1 s?

TRANSPORTATION

2. Change the acceleration to 1.6 and press [enter]. This is the value for the acceleration due to gravity on the moon, 1.6 m/s².

a) Describe how the velocity and distance at 1 s differ from on Earth.

3. Change the acceleration to 25 and press [enter]. This is the value for the acceleration due to gravity on Jupiter, 25 m/s².

a) Compare the velocity and distance at 1 s with the values for the moon and Earth.

FOR YOU TO READ

Forces on Falling Objects

On Earth, objects accelerate at a constant rate of 9.8 m/s². The same object, dropped on the surface of the moon, would accelerate at 1.60 m/s². The difference can be explained by the greater gravitational attraction exerted by the greater mass of planet Earth. However, in air, an additional force acts on falling objects. Molecules strike the falling object, slowing its descent. The friction caused by air molecules is often called drag. This helps explain why a flat piece of paper floats to the ground, while one crumpled into a ball falls at a much faster speed. The greater the surface area (such as for the flat paper), the greater is the drag. As objects move through the air they collide with air molecules. The drag force depends upon the size and shape of the object, the density of the air, and the speed of motion.

If you drop a ball, it has very little velocity at the beginning of its descent, and therefore, it will have little drag force. As the ball increases in velocity, the drag force increases. At some time during the descent the drag force will equal the gravitational force. The net force is now zero and the ball falls with a constant velocity (it no longer accelerates). This is referred to as the terminal velocity.

Falling objects		Terminal Velocity
	ping-pong ball	9 m/s
	baseball	20 m/s
	sky diver in spread eagle	60 m/s
	parachute open	5 m/s

Objects that move in space do not strike air molecules. Molecules within the atmosphere are held by the Earth's gravitational attraction. As you move away from planet Earth, its gravitational force decreases and there are fewer air molecules that will collide with a spacecraft.

REFLECTING ON THE ACTIVITY OR THE CHALLENGE

Sometimes everyday observations do not appear to be supported by scientific theories. You have observed that objects which have a large flat surface often fall more slowly than objects that appear to be more streamline. For example, a feather appears to fall more slowly than a bowling ball. Yet Newton's physics indicates that mass does not affect that speed at which objects fall. Non-science writers often have difficulties linking everyday observations with scientific explanations. In many cases they abandon scientific theories when they do not support observations.

To explain this inconsistency, consider the fact that as objects move through the atmosphere, they strike molecules of air. Not surprisingly, the shape of the object affects how many molecules it strikes as it falls. Each molecule that strikes a falling object exerts a force on the falling object. Even a small force affects an object in motion. The friction caused by the air molecules, referred to as drag, helps explain why some objects fall more slowly than others. Review your story once again to see why some everyday explanations appear to conflict with scientific theories. How could you maintain the scientific theory and still account for the everyday observation?

PHYSICS TO GO

1. Does a feather fall as quickly as a baseball?

2. Would you be able to throw a baseball farther on Earth or Jupiter? Explain your answer.

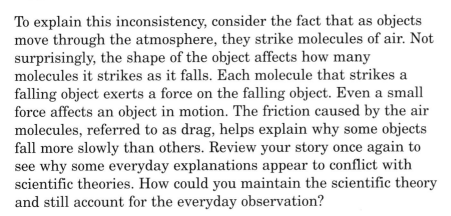

3. Arrange the diagrams so that the scales are arranged from lowest weight to greatest weight.

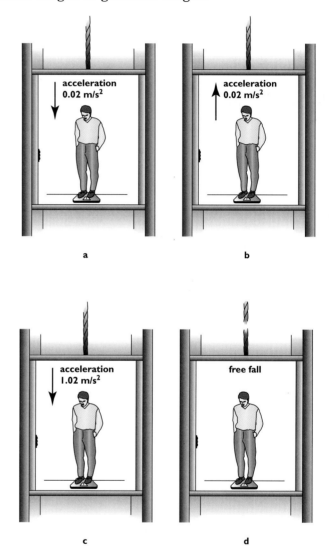

4. Velcro was used to hold objects in place on the space shuttle. Why might objects begin to float around as the shuttle orbits?

STRETCHING EXERCISES

The diagram below shows a devise that is able to measure the acceleration of a falling body.

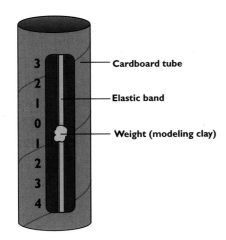

Design and construct an accelerometer that is able to monitor small changes in velocity as might be experienced on the space shuttle.

Activity Four
Life without Gravity

WHAT DO YOU THINK?

Whether you are orbiting Earth in the space shuttle or traveling to the moon or beyond, much of your journey will be in a weightless environment.

• **Why is eating dinner different in a weightless environment?**

Record your ideas about these questions in your *Active Physics log*. Be prepared to discuss your responses with your small group and the class.

FOR YOU TO DO

1. Living in a weightless environment creates problems. Every little detail of daily life works out differently from what is ordinarily expected. Suppose you were in this weightless condition and you tried to lift a spoonful of soup to your mouth. You can lift the soup out of the bowl, because you are accelerating it. When it gets to your lips, you stop the spoon. But the soup doesn't stop. There is nothing to hold it down. It flies off the spoon, rounding up into a perfect sphere as it floats toward the ceiling or toward your forehead.

   Watch the videotape of life situations in a zero gravity condition. As you watch the video, compare each activity you see with what happens on Earth. Then answer the questions below.

   a) Why do the astronauts sleep with their arms in such a strange position?

   b) Why must the astronauts be strapped down onto the treadmill?

   c) What would a person with long hair look like?

2. Choose two of the devices listed below for your group to investigate:

   - a dining table
   - a bed
   - a shower
   - a toilet
   - a clothes closet
   - an exercise machine

   a) Describe in detail the standard Earth-gravity version of the device.

   b) List the problems that the standard version of that device would have in zero-gravity conditions.

   c) What innovative solution can you propose? How will it work in zero gravity?

   d) Be prepared to present your ideas to the other groups. As you compare results, try to reach a consensus about the best way to deal with these problems.

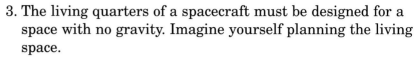

3. The living quarters of a spacecraft must be designed for a space with no gravity. Imagine yourself planning the living space.

   a) List all the details that must be thought of when planning a living space.

   b) Get together with a committee to design some ordinary living arrangements in a zero-gravity environment. Remember that space is severely limited, and you would like to make things as comfortable as possible. Your design will be graded on whether it provides the most comfort and the best living conditions, and whether it uses the least amount of space possible.

REFLECTING ON THE ACTIVITY OR THE CHALLENGE

The human body was designed to work properly in a world of gravity. Where there is no gravity, the body suffers. About half of all astronauts are nauseous a lot of the time. Does this surprise you? Imagine what it would be like to spend days and months on the fastest downhill slope of a roller coaster. That's what it feels like. If the astronauts stay without gravity for an extended length of time, they suffer from weakened bones and muscles, changes in the pattern of blood circulation, and many other physical problems.

Think once again about your science-fiction story. How will you describe the variety of problems for astronauts presented by little or no gravity? How will the use of toilets and showers be different on your journey? Part of your story can involve descriptions of the living spaces and contrasts between everyday life on a spacecraft and everyday life on Earth. In the For You To Read section which follows, you can find out about the impact of colors in the furniture and walls of the spacecraft. You may want to include color design into part of your story. Another article which follows describes the need for exercise machines to be vibration free. The daily exercise of the astronauts could be another addition to your story line. You will learn more about exercise in the next activity.

FOR YOU TO READ

Interior Color Testing for Space Station Freedom

Reprinted from *Station Break* (Vol. 4, No. 12, Dec. 1992).

With hundreds of thousands of technical details being determined about Space Station Freedom, one might think the colors used inside would be among the last concerns. But that's not so. In fact some very scientific and detailed testing is under way to select the best color schemes for the space station.

And it's much more than just what looks best. There are many considerations in choosing the space station's colors. Light reflection and absorption, the durability of the finish, integration with the international partners and even the psychological effects are all concerns in color tests.

"What we really are trying to do right now is determine what colors don't work in order to propose some that do," said George Tamas, an industrial designer in Boeing's human-systems division, who has been performing the color testing.

But before colors are determined, other considerations must be made. For instance, the type of finish specified. Although a glossy finish cleans up easily, the glare produced is unacceptable, so a semi-gloss or flat finish will be used. There are also concerns of the paint chipping or flaking, so a two part catalytic paint is needed that will not release unwanted gases into

the space station's environment.

When it comes to lighting, foot-candle readings are taken of different colors to determine the amount of reflection. If a color does not reflect a required amount of light, it will not be considered. If a color reflects more light, that means less power for lighting is needed and that power can be used more efficiently in other areas.

"If we're talking about a 50-watt difference, that could be the difference in turning on an experiment or being able to warm dinner," said Tamas.

Boeing's color testing in the US laboratory and living quarters has been under way for two years now in the space station mock-up at Marshall Space Flight Center in Huntsville. The international partners also are conducting their own color tests for their modules. Because Boeing engineers have twice the space to consider, there is more flexibility in their use of colors.

As for the colors, federal standards must be met. Most of those involve various shades of white, gray, and tan. But if approved, additional colors can be used. For instance, inside the living quarters, the wardroom is being tested in shades of red. Because the racks on the space station can be moved, their design and positioning must also be considered in determining their color.

The idea is to use colors that make sense for the area. In the working environment of the laboratory, lighter colors will be used to enhance

the work environment. Colors that are considered stressful are ruled out. Currently, grays and whites with blue trim are the functional choices. Inside the habitat or "home" for the crew, more cozy, warm colors will be used, giving a sense of security. In the sleeping area, darker, more peaceful shades are the choice.

Gerard Carr, former Skylab astronaut and now a Boeing technical support subcontractor in Huntsville, said coloring is an integral part of Freedom's design. Carr and his fellow crew members spent the longest amount of time yet on an American mission—84 days back in 1973.

"It was like being in the New Mexico or Arizona desert," said Carr. "Everything was finished in earth tones and unexciting, designed not to give any stimulation or distractions."

Carr said based on his Skylab experience, there needs to be some textures also involved in the space station colors.

"The only colors we had on board were the color bars on the wall we used to register the cameras. We really missed color as well as aromas. . .you need the stimulation for a long term in space."

There also is the psychological aspect of choosing the right colors. Great care must be made to avoid eye fatigue, colors that are tiring to look at over time.

Taking Physical Fitness to New Frontiers: Station-Related Cycle Stabilizer to Undergo Shuttle Flight Test

Reprinted from Station Break (Vol. 4, No. 5, May 1992).

A major challenge in designing future manned space missions may now be resolved, thanks to some new equipment developed by NASA and Lockheed.

The challenge is the incompatibility of physical exercise and microgravity science. Astronauts must exercise during their missions, but sensitive microgravity experiments conducted on those missions need a spacecraft environment free from disturbance.

The NASA/Lockheed solution is a platform that supports the exercise equipment yet cancels out

the vibrations, allowing astronauts to work out strenuously without interfering with science experiments. The device is called the Isolated Exercise Platform (ISEP). The first flight-ready stabilized platform was delivered to Johnson Space Center in January. Its Shuttle debut is planned for June, in the middeck of the Space Shuttle Columbia.

Dr. Damon Smith, Lockheed's stabilized platform chief scientist and project leader, said, "It's desirable that astronauts on the longer Shuttle missions perform hard aerobic exercise daily. Without this exercise, the prolonged absence of gravity could affect the crew's ability to stand upright without dizziness when they return to Earth."

Typically, orbiting astronauts have exercised on a bicycle or treadmill mounted to a Shuttle bulkhead. "When there are no sensitive experiments aboard, this is not a problem," Smith said, "but in the presence of microgravity research such as protein crystal growth, this amount of activity interferes. It's important for space station crew members or voyagers to Mars, who also must counteract the prolonged effects of weightlessness on their skeletal systems. Bones lose calcium during long periods without gravity, and exercise is an effective counter-measure to deal with this loss.

"The conflict between the medical need for exercise and the sensitivity of microgravity experiments has challenged space planners for

some time," Smith said. "We think we've solved the problem with the ISEP."

Lockheed designed the first stabilized platform for use with an ergometer, a stationary-cycle device built by the European Space Agency. Future designs will accommodate a treadmill and a rowing machine.

The June flight of Columbia will be STS-50, a 13-day microgravity research mission called United States Microgravity Laboratory 1. USML-1 will be the longest Space Shuttle flight to date. Crew exercise is a top priority.

"TV viewers worldwide may be able to look in as the astronauts go through their daily exercise regimen on the ergometer, which will be mounted on Lockheed's ISEP," Smith said.

The stabilized platform consists of four rectangular stabilizers attached vertically to a frame, which rests on shock absorbers called isolators. The ergometer attaches to the frame. The stabilizers hold each corner of the frame stationary. Smith explained, "A motor inside each stabilizer uses inertial stabilization to counteract the disturbances caused by the exercise."

Without stabilizers, a crewmember peddling a stationary bicycle can produce as much as 100 pounds of force, which far exceeds the allowable microgravity disturbance limits set by NASA.

With Lockheed's stabilized platform system, the exercise is expected to cause less than one pound of disturbance force on the Shuttle middeck.

From concept to delivery, Lockheed produced the flight equipment very quickly. Smith said, "We came up with the design only last year and, in about nine months, built, tested and shipped the hardware to Johnson Space Center. We certainly believe this product meets the requirements of NASA's microgravity and life-sciences offices. The successful use of stabilized platforms on USML-1 will show that the needs of both the crew and the microgravity scientists can be accomodated simultaneously on the same spacecraft."

Smith's group is part of the Space Station Freedom office at Lockheed.

PHYSICS TO GO

1. Look up the inside dimensions of the Apollo command module, the space shuttle, or MIR. Calculate the volume per person. Measure your room at home and calculate the volume per person. Compare them.

2. Read the article on page T137, "Interior Color Testing for Space Station Freedom" from *Station Break* (Vol. 4, No. 12, Dec. 1992). Is selecting a paint scheme and composition for a space station very different from doing that for a home or school? Can you make any suggestions for your school based on the NASA findings?

3. Read the article on page T138, "Taking Physical Fitness to New Frontiers" from *Station Break* (Vol. 4, No. 5, May 1992). Describe the two conflicting problems that were solved by the new cycle. What problems might the new cycle introduce to space shuttle designers in the future?

4. Two candles were lit and the flame was observed. How might the observations differ if this demonstration was carried out in a microgravity environment? *(Hint: Would the flame "know" which way is "up" in zero gravity?)*

STRETCHING EXERCISES

Soak 4 bean seeds in water overnight and then position the seedlings in a Petri dish that has been filled with soaking, paper towels. Store the dish in a dark place in the position shown in the diagram.

a) Check the seedling after 5 and 10 days and describe the movement of the roots and stems?
b) Explain your results.
c) Hypothesize how the experimental results would change had this experiment been conducted in a microgravity environment, such as a space shuttle.

Activity Five

Excercise on the Moon

WHAT DO YOU THINK?

You have often heard that there is no gravity or less gravity on the moon.

- **Why do you think that this is true?**
- **What would account for less gravity or no gravity on the moon?**

Record your ideas about these questions in your *Active Physics log*. Be prepared to discuss your responses with your small group and the class.

FOR YOU TO DO

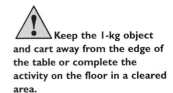

1. Attach a 1-kg object and suspend it from a force meter (a spring scale). You are measuring the force that the Earth's gravity exerts on the object. This is called the weight of the object.

   a) How much does the 1-kg object weigh?

2. Put the kilogram mass on a low-friction lab cart. Attach a force meter. The weight of the object is now completely supported by the cart. Attach the force meter, by way of a string, to the cart. Pull in a horizontal direction, so that you get the cart and 1-kg object moving horizontally. The force meter now says nothing at all about the weight of the standard.

⚠️ **Keep the 1-kg object and cart away from the edge of the table or complete the activity on the floor in a cleared area.**

   a) When you pull the cart horizontally, you are accelerating the object by exerting a force on it. How much force?

   b) Can you vary the force?

   c) What happens if you increase the force?

When the object is suspended from a force meter and only the meter and gravity act on the object, the force meter measures its weight. When you accelerate the object, the force used depends on the object's mass, and on how much acceleration you give it. In this situation, $F = ma$.

3. View the videotape of astronauts walking around and jumping on the moon. Also see the film of Neil Armstrong dropping a hammer and a feather.

   a) What do these films tell you about the conditions on the moon?

TRANSPORTATION

4. If you can lift a 60-lb. object on Earth, you can lift a 360-lb. object on the moon! This seems like a wonderful advantage. It also has some real problems. If you weigh 150 lbs. on Earth, your leg muscles are used to carrying around 150 lbs. all day long, every day. You give your legs exercise every day by just standing around and having your legs hold up 150 lbs. On the moon, you will weigh only $\frac{1}{6}$ as much or 25 lbs. As you stand on the moon, your legs will only be holding up 25 lbs. What will happen to your muscles? The effects of low gravity cause your muscles and bones to weaken. Exercise is the key.

In your group, decide on an exercise program that will keep a person's muscles fit so that when the space traveler returns to Earth after a long journey, she will be able to stand and walk around. Pushing 100 kg on the moon is just as difficult as pushing 100 kg on the Earth. Lifting 100 kg on the moon is much, much easier than lifting 100 kg on Earth.

a) Identify the different muscle groups of the body that you will be exercising.

b) Record the exercise program in your log.

c) Compare your moon exercise regimen with an exercise regimen on Earth.

PHYSICS TALK

Newton's Second Law of Motion

Newton related mass, acceleration, and force in what has become know as his Second Law of Motion. Part of this law states:

The acceleration of an object is directly proportional to the unbalanced force acting on it and inversely proportional to the object's mass.

This equation can be written in three possible forms:

$$F = ma \qquad a = \frac{F}{m} \qquad m = \frac{F}{a}$$

where F is the force expressed in newtons (N), a is the acceleration expressed in meters per second squared (m/s^2), and m is the mass measured in kilograms (kg).

FOR YOU TO READ

Acceleration Due to Gravity on Earth and on the Moon

If you ever get to the moon, you will have to carry around a life-support pack that you could not even lift when you were back home on Earth. It will not be a great burden on the moon. Yet, there is just as much material in that pack when you lift it on the moon as there was when it was loaded into the spacecraft.

On the moon, the mass of all objects is identical to the mass of those objects on Earth. The acceleration due to gravity is considerably less on the moon and objects weigh less. While the hammer and the feather dropped together on the video made on the moon, they did not accelerate downward at 9.8 m/s^2. The acceleration was only 1.6 m/s^2. This low acceleration due to gravity also accounts for the way the astronauts seem almost to float as they walk around.

	Earth	Moon
Acceleration due to gravity	9.8 m/s^2	1.6 m/s^2

How to Tell Mass from Weight

Mass and weight are often confused, but they are quite different. One reason for the confusion is that the same unit is often used for both. When you use the unit "pound," sometimes you are talking about weight and sometimes about mass. In the SI system (the international system of units), weight is a force, so it is measured in the SI force unit, newton. Mass is measured in kilograms.

To make the difference clear, think of the following situation. You are preparing a potato salad for 100 people. About 50 pounds of potatoes will make salad for 100 people. You go to the supermarket and buy a 50-pound bag of potatoes. It is a strain to lift it, but you manage. (When you think about the difficulty of lifting the bag of potatoes, are you thinking about its mass or its weight?) Now suppose you were making the potato salad on the moon. Do you agree that the 50-pound bag of potatoes will still feed 100 people on the moon? The amount of substance in them is the same as on Earth; they have the same mass. When you lift up the bag, however, it is very light. It is no strain at all to get it onto your shoulder. While its mass is the same, it weighs only about 8 pounds. Weight is the force of gravity acting on something. The moon's gravity is much weaker than the Earth's. Everything feels lighter on the moon because the gravitational pull is less than on Earth.

REFLECTING ON THE ACTIVITY AND THE CHALLENGE

Understanding the effects of the lower gravitational attraction by the moon is important for your story. Lifting objects on the moon will be different from pulling them. Because the gravitational pull is $\frac{1}{6}$ that of Earth, you would be able to lift 6 times the weight on the moon. Just think of the things that you could accomplish! Imagine how you might change a tire on a vehicle.

Also think about how an extended stay on the moon would affect you when you returned to Earth. Because your body weight on the moon has been reduced by a fraction of $\frac{1}{6}$, your muscles are placed under less strain. A musculature and skeleton that must support 150 lbs. on Earth needs to support only 25 lbs. on the moon. Not surprisingly, a skeletal system and muscles which are used much less begin to weaken. Bones that are less dense and a reduced muscle mass will present many problems for a person who returns to Earth. The amount of exercise that you do while recovering must be controlled.

Check your story once again. Have you accounted for short term and long term adjustments to lower gravity? How could you use this principle to make your story even more interesting? Consider the possibilities of doing athletic training on a planet with increased or reduced gravitational force.

PHYSICS TO GO

1. Why does it take a tremendous booster rocket to accelerate a space craft off Earth, but a much smaller rocket to produce the acceleration to get it off the moon. Use Newton's Second Law ($F = ma$) in explaining your answer.

2. Suppose that you lived in a lunar colony. Describe how the difference in weight, but not mass, would affect an everyday activity such as housework, recreation, etc.

3. On Jupiter, gravity is almost 3 times stronger than on Earth (everything weighs 3 times as much on Jupiter). Answer question 2 as if you were in a base on Jupiter.

4. If you were a high jumper, what benefits would be achieved by:

   a) training on Jupiter?
   b) holding the competition on the moon?

5. You must allocate enough fuel to escape the gravitational attraction of the body that it rests upon.

   a) Would more fuel be used by a spaceship to leave planet Earth or the moon? Explain your answer.
   b) In what ways would the allocation of fuel be different if a return trip was to be considered between Earth and Jupiter, rather than between Earth and the moon.
   c) How would docking a spaceship on the moon be different from docking it on Jupiter? Which do you believe would be more difficult? Explain your answer.

6. On Earth determining mass is simple. A spring balance or bathroom scale can be used because gravity is a constant. Measuring mass in space presents a much greater challenge. How would you know if astronauts were receiving the needed nutrition and neither gaining or losing weight?

7. How many different exercise machines would be needed to exercise all of the muscle groups? How could they all fit in the limited space of the ship?

Activity Six
The Necessities of Life

WHAT DO YOU THINK?

In order to survive in space, you must take with you all the substances and materials needed to support life. One of these substances is the oxygen you breathe. When a manned space flight is planned, space and weight allowances for these necessities must go into the calculations.

- **How much do you think the oxygen needed to support you for one week weighs?**
- **Could you supply this oxygen by bringing plants with you on your trip?**

Record your ideas about these questions in your *Active Physics log*. Be prepared to discuss your responses with your small group and the class.

FOR YOU TO DO

1. Count the number of times your lab partner exhales in one minute while at rest and then in one minute after three minutes of vigorous exercise (i.e. running in place).

a) Record the values in your log.

b) Complete at least three trials for each situation and calculate the average. Make a table similar to the following. Record the average under the heading breaths/min, for rest and exercise.

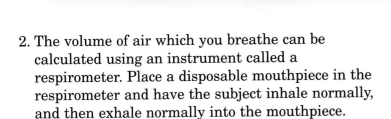

Activity	Breaths/min	Volume/breath mL	Volume/min mL/min
rest			
exercise			

2. The volume of air which you breathe can be calculated using an instrument called a respirometer. Place a disposable mouthpiece in the respirometer and have the subject inhale normally, and then exhale normally into the mouthpiece.

If a commercial respirometer is not available, you may use the apparatus shown in the diagram. Ensure that the rubber tubing is disinfected by alcohol and not used by more than one subject.

a) Record the volume of air exhaled in the volume/breath column for "rest." It represents a normal exhalation at rest.

3. Ask the subject to take a maximum inhalation and then exhale as much as possible into the mouthpiece.

a) Record this value in the volume/breath column for exercise. It represents the maximum air movement during times of extreme exercise.

4. Use the information you obtained in this activity to calculate the following.

a) Analysis indicates that air entering the lung contains 21% oxygen, while the air leaving the lung contains 14% oxygen. Indicate how much oxygen is used each minute while at rest, and during excercise.

b) The volume of air in a space craft is about the same as in an ordinary bedroom measuring 3 m long × 4 m wide × 3 m high. (1 m³ of gas = 1000 L = 1,000,000 mL) Calculate the amount of oxygen available to the astronauts.

5. In sunlight, green plants produce oxygen. Would it be possible for the astronauts to supply their oxygen needs by bringing a supply of plants with them? You will need the following information to help you answer this question:

- The amount of air a person breathes every hour (calculate this from your experimental data)

- Air is only 21% oxygen.

- In your lungs, $\frac{1}{3}$ of the oxygen in each breath actually gets into the cells of the body.

- In full sunlight, a green plant emits about 2 L of oxygen per hour for each square meter of leaf surface.

Now you are in a position to answer some questions:

a) How many liters of oxygen does a person use every hour?

b) How much leaf surface area would be needed to make oxygen at this rate, in bright light?

c) Are green plants a practical solution to the oxygen problem?

REFLECTING ON THE ACTIVITY AND CHALLENGE

On Earth you take the exchange of gases for granted. Humans use oxygen and exhale carbon dioxide. Plants, through photosynthesis, exchange the carbon dioxide for oxygen, thereby replenishing the oxygen supply. Supplying astronauts with oxygen is but one of the problems that faces space scientists. As the astronaut exhales, carbon dioxide is released. In low concentrations, carbon dioxide does not create a problem, but as the concentration increases breathing rate will increase. At very high concentrations carbon dioxide will become toxic. The greatest danger that met the ill-fated Apollo 13 was removing the excess carbon dioxide.

The problem of life support becomes more difficult as more astronauts are included on a ship and as they are kept in space longer. Not only do they need oxygen, but the water vapor and carbon dioxide produced during respiration must be removed. Astronauts also need food, water, warmth, and a means to dispose of what goes into the toilets. Also, not only must the necessities for life be transported in a space craft, but the containers that carry them as well.

Look at your story. In 2001, astronauts were frozen to save on food and oxygen. What other solutions exist for saving these necessities on a long journey? What happens if oxygen levels get low? Can some of the potential problems make for a good science-fiction story? How will you realistically account for all the necessities of life? What part of your story is fiction?

PHYSICS TO GO

1. Find the approximate value for the weight of food and fluids you consume in one day. Use this to calculate the approximate weight of the food and water needed to support four astronauts for one week.

2. Design the perfect food for astronauts. Take into consideration all that you learned, and think about keeping nutritive value high and resulting waste low. Would you enjoy eating this food?

3. Water loss is one of the greatest problems faced by astronauts doing extended space travel. What suggestions could you make that would help astronauts:

   a) conserve water.
   b) recycle water.

4. Make an estimate of the amount of water that you use daily for things other than eating. Brushing your teeth, washing your hands, washing dishes, showers, and the toilet account for a tremendous usage of water. Explain how your daily activities would be changed if your personal water supply was decreased by 90%.

5. Carbon dioxide levels must be controlled during spaceflight. In order to reduce carbon dioxide levels in a space station, a commander rules that only one hour of exercise is permitted daily. Would you agree with the proposed solution? Give your reasons.

STRETCHING EXERCISES

1. NASA has a wealth of available information about space travel. Contact a NASA station for literature that describes the containers for packing food, oxygen, etc., for astronauts to live in space or on a shuttle.
2. Contact a NASA station for literature about design plans for a space colony and long-term missions to the moon or Mars.
3. Read about the Apollo 13 mission and detail the problems involved with gas exchange systems.

Activity Seven

Communication

WHAT DO YOU THINK?

Picture yourself as an astronaut on a spacewalk. You are all alone, floating around in infinite space. No other human being in the history of the world has ever been so alone.

- **Could you use a loudspeaker to communicate with the space ship while on a spacewalk?**

Record your ideas about these questions in your *Active Physics log*. Be prepared to discuss your responses with your small group and the class.

FOR YOU TO DO

1. Connect a bell jar by a hose to a vacuum pump, as shown in the diagram. Put a doorbell inside the bell jar, and start it ringing. Turn on the pump and listen as nearly all the air is removed from the bell jar.

  a) What happens to the sound you hear as the air is removed?

  b) The space between an astronaut on a space walk and the space ship is totally empty. There is no air at all. Based on your observations, can an astronaut on a spacewalk communicate through a loudspeaker? Explain your answer.

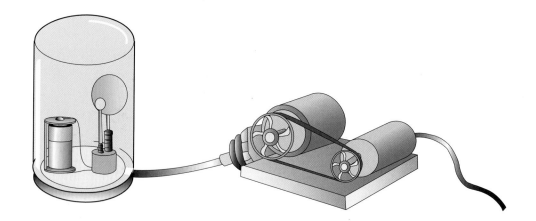

2. Have your partner sit with eyes closed. Snap your fingers above your partner's head. Keep your fingers an equal distance from each of your partner's ears each time you snap your fingers. Snap your fingers in several locations from the front to the back of the head. Ask your partner to guess where your fingers are located.

  a) Record in your log where your fingers were located, and if your partner was able to correctly identify the position.

3. Repeat step 2, but this time snap your fingers in a variety of different directions from the ears.

   a) Invent a way to indicate and measure the accuracy of your partner's identification. Describe your measurement technique in your log.

   b) From the result of the activity was your partner able to determine the direction from which a sound was coming?

   c) When was it most difficult to determine the direction of a sound?

4. Repeat steps 3 for different distances.

5. Using the sound of snapping fingers or a tapping noise, carefully guide your partner, eyes still closed, around an area determined by your teacher.

   a) In addition to understanding speech, how else do you use sound and your sense of hearing?

FOR YOU TO READ

Sound is the movement of molecules caused by a vibrating body. Sound travels in waves. The nature of sound became clearer after an experiment by Robert Boyle in 1660. Boyle wondered whether sound could be produced in a vacuum. A watch with an alarm was suspended in a bell jar. The alarm was set and air was then pumped out of the bell jar. Boyle watched as the time that he set the alarm for approached, but to his amazement the alarm could not be heard. Sound must travel through a medium. Air is the most common medium, but sound travels through other media. Sound travels through water (1480 m/sec at 20°C) four times faster than air (370 m/sec at 20°C). Solids, because molecules are even more densely arranged, transmit sound even more rapidly than liquids do. Sound travels in steel at a speed of 6100 m/sec.

REFLECTING ON THE ACTIVITY AND THE CHALLENGE

Anyone who has seen the movie *Star Wars* has seen spacecraft explode in deep space with a thunderous roar. However, the roar would never be heard. Although the thunderous explosion is more dramatic than just a flash of light, it contributes to the misunderstandings people have about space travel. Good science fiction must be plausible. Many movies and television shows that deal with science fiction employ scientists as consultants. Identify correct and incorrect statements in your science fiction story involving sound. What changes would you have to make to your story to make it more believable?

In this activity, you found that the ability to hear sound also helps you determine your whereabouts and gain some knowledge about your surroundings. How could you use this fact to make a scene in a science fiction story both realistic and exciting? You will find out more about communication in space in the next activity.

PHYSICS TO GO

1. In this activity would you be able hear the alarm clock better if the bell jar was filled with water? Assume that water does not affect any electrical mechanism in the alarm clock.

2. In many science fiction movies scenes of explosions in outer space are accompanied by loud sounds. Explain what is wrong about such a scene.

3. As a spaceship moves away from Earth would sound become more or less intense? Give your reasons.

4. Explain why people aboard a space station can hear each other speak.

5. Assume that a species of human-like animals can live on the moon without requiring a space suit. Would you expect them to speak softly or yell at one another to be heard? Give your reasons.

Activity Eight

The Speed of Radio Waves

WHAT DO YOU THINK?

A radio station at one end of your time zone transmits a signal that says, "At the tone, the time will be exactly 3 P.M. — beep!" The signal travels up to an orbiting geosynchronous satellite, and then back down to your radio receiver, a round trip of 50,000 miles.

• **If you live at the other end of the time zone, what time would it be when you hear the signal?**

• **If you asked an astronaut on the moon a question, how much time would elapse before you heard her response on Earth?**

Record your ideas about these questions in your *Active Physics log*. Be prepared to discuss your responses with your small group and the class.

TRANSPORTATION

FOR YOU TO DO

1. You can use a simple system to explore some of the properties of the radio waves that astronauts use to communicate. Such waves are produced any time an electric spark jumps. You can produce radio waves with a simple spark generator. The best way to detect those waves is with an ordinary AM radio, tuned between stations.

   Use a spark generator at one end of the room to make a spark while you listen to the radio on the other end of the room. Have a partner turn the spark on and off.

   🖊 a) What do you hear at the spark generator, and at the radio? Are the two sounds the same?

2. Test whether the radio wave will pass through a vacuum by putting the spark generator inside a bell jar and pump out the air using a vacuum pump.

   🖊 a) When the air is pumped out, can you still hear the sound of the spark?

   🖊 b) Can you still hear the sound coming out of the radio?

   🖊 c) What does this tell you about the difference between sound waves and radio waves?

   🖊 d) Write a statement giving your conclusions about the ability of radio waves to pass through a vacuum.

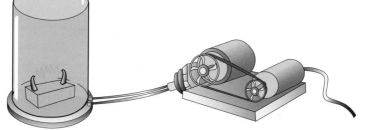

3. Radio waves travel very quickly. If you have ever used a walkie-talkie, you found that the signal seemed to travel to the other walkie-talkies in no time at all. What would happen if the distance between the two walkie-talkies is extremely large, would it be possible to detect a time delay?

Watch a segment of the NASA film showing communication with astronauts on the moon. When a communication is received, an astronaut is supposed to answer "roger" immediately.

✎ a) Why is there a noticeable delay in the arrival of the answer? Could it be that astronauts do not think as fast on the moon?

4. From the film, you can get an estimate of the speed of travel of a radio signal. Look again at the sequence in which the astronauts on the moon are answering a signal from Earth. When you get the transmission from Earth, answer "roger." Now estimate the time delay between your "roger" and the response from the moon. This is the length of time it took the signal to get to the moon and back. Repeat this until you feel you have a good estimate of the time delay.

✎ a) Record the time delay in your log.

✎ b) Calculate the speed of the signal. The distance to the moon is about 243,000 miles, or 3.80×10^8 m.

REFLECTING ON THE ACTIVITY AND THE CHALLENGE

The fact that radio waves move through a vacuum and that sound waves don't provides an excellent clue as to why communication in deep space uses radio waves. You may want to incorporate some aspect of communication over distance into your story.

Many science fiction movies use earth-bound examples to construct scenarios about communications in space. The delay in receiving and transmitting radio waves over great distances creates problems for the astronauts. The greater the distance, the greater is the delay. Think of how these short delays would affect a crisis situation. You may want to include this feature in your story. This also presents an opportunity to annotate some examples of why the delays are not used. Would the delay slow the delivery of the plot?

FOR YOU TO READ

Electromagnetic Waves

When Heinrich Hertz first demonstrated the existence of radio waves in 1886, he had no idea that they would turn out to be useful. He was interested only in advancing knowledge of electricity and magnetism. By 1901, knowledge of radio waves had progressed so far that Guglielmo Marconi was able to send a coded signal across the Atlantic Ocean.

Today, these same electromagnetic waves carry radio and television signals. They are used to communicate with satellites and to see objects in the far reaches of outer space. In a microwave oven, they cook your food. Radar determines the exact position of airplanes approaching an airport. A transmitter attached to an eagle enables a biologist to follow its movements.

What else do you know that travels at about the speed of radio waves? The accepted value for the speed of radio waves is 300,000,000 (3×10^8) m/s, or 186,000 miles per second. This is commonly known as the speed of light. At that speed, a radio signal could get from London to New York in a couple of hundredths of a second. All electromagnetic waves—light, ultraviolet, infrared, radio, microwave—travel at this speed.

Sound is not an electromagnetic wave, and does not travel at the speed of such waves. The difference between the speed of sound and the speed of light is apparent whenever you see and hear something that happens at a distance. If you are sitting high up in the stadium to watch a baseball game, you see the ball well on its way before you hear the crack of the bat. Watching target practice from a distance, you see the barrel smoke before you hear the sound of the gun.

Can you think of other examples?

PHYSICS TO GO

1. Find the distances to Mars, Jupiter, the nearest star, and the nearest galaxy. Calculate how long a radio signal would take to travel to these locations. Would conversations with a space traveler be practical in these contexts?

2. If extraterrestrial life were discovered on a planetary system near a star close to Earth, the answer to a question may require 50 years. You would certainly want to have a decent conversation with this intelligent life form. How could you carry out a meaningful conversation given that the radio signal takes so long to get there and back?

3. Explain why radio waves could be used to determine the distance of distant stars.

4. Are there any other technologies around that might be used for communication in years to come?

5. What are the limitations of radio communication and what can be done about them? Why is cable TV used?

6. Is there any limit to the amount of radio communication, that can be used at any time, and what can be done about it?

7. In what ways would modern life be different if you had no access to radio waves?

INQUIRY INVESTIGATION

Find some other properties of radio waves. Use the spark generator and the AM radio. Some of the things you might like to investigate may be:

• How far can the signal from the spark generator be detected? inside the school building? outdoors?

• Can radio waves go through a wall?

• Can radio waves go around the corner of a building?

• Can the radio wave carry the signal through the metal of a can?

Decide on what procedures you will use, and submit them to your teacher for approval. Carry out your investigation.

Write a statement giving your conclusions about the ability of radio waves to pass through a vacuum, around corners, through metal, across distances, etc.

PHYSICS AT WORK

George Takei

SET A COURSE FOR THE FUTURE MR. SULU

George Takei, as Lt. Sulu, is one of the original Star Trek characters from the television series that began in the late 1960s. He has become, as all the early Star Trek characters have, a science fiction icon.

George believes that imagination and inquisitiveness are the most important factors that move society ahead. And, Star Trek clearly represents that visionary imagination. "Science fiction," claims George "can become fact if we let our imaginations free, free to ask—what if."

"When Star Trek was first conceived by Gene Rodenbury," George explains, "we had scientists from the Rand Corporation to help guide and stimulate our writers and production teams. Gene was a visionary, but he knew that he had to reconcile any problems that might come up between science fiction and science fact."

"Science fiction is a wonderful vehicle to envision new possibilities for society." states George. "And," he continues, "Gene Roddenbury was a true pioneer. He had strong views about human civilization and he created the Starship Enterprise to represent that vision. The Starship Enterprise became a metaphor for the Starship Earth. The bridge of our starship was populated with a wide cultural diversity. At that time on television, it was revolutionary to see that kind of cultural diversity celebrated. In the role that I had the privilege to play, for example, it was the first time that an Asian was depicted on television in an non-servile, non-clownish, non-villain type role. Lt. Sulu was a capable, professional part of the leadership team on the bridge of the Enterprise."

George has written one science fiction novel himself and he explains, "when you write science fiction you have the freedom to create through your imagination another world, a world with its own social and physical reality." He also points out that often what was once considered science fiction later becomes science fact. For example, in 1969, during Star Trek's second season, a man landed on the moon for the first time. "For us on the Starship Enterprise that was rather old hat. We had been 'beaming down' to moons and other planet surfaces for quite a while."

Chapter 3 Assessment

Now that you have finished this chapter, it is time to complete your challenge. You are trying to help my little brother, or any other young sci-fi fan, learn the difference between science fact and science fiction. You may have already started writing a story, and you probably have a number of new and exciting ideas to include.

- **Complete writing your science-fiction story about a trip to the moon or beyond.**

- **In a separate key to your story (an annotation), explain where the science is true and where you have modified the physics for interest or excitement.**

Review the criteria that you agreed on at the beginning of the chapter. Your criteria may have included the following:

- **the maximum and minimum length of the story and annotation;**

- **how much of the grade should depend on creativity and interest in the story;**

- **how much should depend on the annotation that relates and describes the real physics in your story and your modifications of physics;**

- **how many physics concepts you should include to receive an "A" for your work.**

Read over your story. Should it be modified at this point?

Physics You Learned

Free fall

Weight

Apparent weight

Weightlessness

Mass and weight

Technology in zero gravity

$F = ma$

Fermi problem—oxygen use

Sound in vacuum

Radio wave transmission in a vacuum

Speed of radio waves

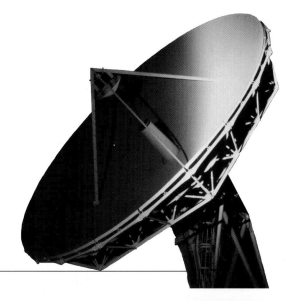

Index